The Design of Coffee
An Engineering Approach

Second Edition

William Ristenpart & Tonya Kuhl

Department of Chemical Engineering, University of California Davis

Ristenpart / Kuhl Publishing

2016

Acknowledgments – We thank the many individuals and organizations who have enthusiastically supported the development of *The Design of Coffee*, including the Specialty Coffee Association of America, VST Inc., Rogers Family Coffee, Tony's Coffee, Mishka's Coffee, Chocolate Fish Coffee, Kalita USA, Bunn-o-Matic Corporation, and Peet's Coffee and Tea. We are especially grateful for the generous financial support of Chevron Corporation and the College of Engineering at University of California Davis for supporting the renovation of the Coffee Lab in 2015. There are many individuals from the coffee industry who have been extremely helpful, but we especially acknowledge the assistance of Nicholas Cho of Wrecking Ball Coffee and Peter Giuliano from the Specialty Coffee Association of America. At UC Davis, we are especially indebted to Dr. Bill Doering, both for his excellent management of the Coffee Lab and for his thoughtful advice, suggestions, and critical review of the manuscript, and to Kaitlin Johnson for her superb work as head teaching assistant.

Most of all, we thank the many students who have taken the course and helped us hone the labs – this project would not have been possible without you.

The Design of Coffee: An Engineering Approach

Copyright © 2016, 2015 by William Ristenpart & Tonya Kuhl

All rights reserved. This book or any portion thereof may not be reproduced or used in any manner whatsoever without the express written permission of the publisher except for the use of brief quotations in a book review or scholarly journal.

Cover design by Isabella Perez

Ristenpart / Kuhl Publishing
1 Shields Ave
Davis, CA 95616 USA

ISBN: 1537305573
ISBN-13: 978-1537305578

Preface

This book is intended for use in the laboratory component of "The Design of Coffee," a general education science and engineering course developed at the University of California Davis. Specifically, the course serves as a non-mathematical introduction to chemical engineering as elucidated by the process of roasting and brewing coffee. The primary focus of the course is a weekly 2-hour lab session where students perform experiments designed to illustrate key chemical engineering principles. As described in this book, students learn about material balances, chemical kinetics, mass transfer, conservation of energy, and colloidal phenomena – all examined through the prism of roasting and brewing coffee. Toward the end of the course, the students compete in a design competition where they strive to make the *best* tasting coffee using the *least* amount of energy – a classic engineering optimization problem, but one that is both fun and broadly accessible to a general audience.

"The Design of Coffee" was originally intended for non-science majors who would like to satisfy their general education requirements for science and engineering. Over the past few years, however, we have found that a much larger audience is eager to learn how to think more scientifically about the beverage that they consume on a regular basis. Although this book is primarily intended to serve those students enrolled in "The Design of Coffee," the material and experiments presented here will be of use to anybody interested in learning more about coffee – or how to think about coffee like an engineer.

Accordingly, we have made the material here as self-contained as possible. Anybody at the college freshmen level or above can perform the experiments described here: no calculus or chemistry is required. Importantly, most of the requisite equipment and supplies, such as hot-air popcorn roasters, drip brewers, and green coffee beans, are inexpensive and readily purchased. All of the experiments described here can be performed in a kitchen or anywhere else with access to a sink and electricity.

This new and improved second edition incorporates many improvements that we have implemented over the past year, including a new segment on traditional cupping (in Lab 0) and considerable streamlining of all of the labs. We also have added new bonus material on decaffeination, production of instant coffee, and sustainability issues in coffee.

As with the first edition, an important aspect of this guidebook is that we *don't* provide the answers here to many of the questions we pose. The intent is to have students think about and experimentally explore the underlying physical and chemical processes for themselves using the scientific method, rather than simply reading the answer. Our goal is to help you understand how to think like an engineer – and along the way learn how to make excellent coffee!

William Ristenpart & Tonya Kuhl

Davis, California
Summer 2016

Contents

Preliminaries

    Introduction – Why Coffee & Chemical Engineering?   1

    Equipment and Supplies – What Do We Need?   6

    Lab 0 – Safety Overview and Introduction to Tasting Coffee   9

Part I – Analysis of Coffee

    Lab 1 – Reverse Engineering a Drip Coffee Brewer   19

    Lab 2 – Process Flow Diagram and Mass Balances for Coffee   28

    Lab 3 – The pH of Coffee and Chemical Reactions   36

    Lab 4 – Measuring the Energy Used to Make Coffee   44

    Lab 5 – Mass Transfer and Flux during Brewing   55

    Lab 6 – Coffee as a Colloidal Fluid and the Effect of Filtration   65

Part II – Design of Coffee

    Design Competition Format, Guidelines, & Video Project   78

    Lab 7 – First Design Trials: Optimizing Strength & Extraction   81

    Lab 8 – Second Design Trials: Scaling Up to 1 Liter of Coffee   92

    Lab 9 – Design Competition and Blind Taste Panel   100

Appendix A – General Guidelines for Brewing   107

Appendix B – Useful Units and Conversions for Coffee   108

Appendix C – Tips on Data Analysis & Plotting   109

Further Reading   111

Introduction – Why Coffee and Chemical Engineering?

A cup of coffee

Every morning, millions of people wake up and perform a familiar ritual. Perhaps a bit bleary-eyed and groggy, they make their way to the kitchen and stand in front of a drip coffee maker. There, they launch into a series of well-practiced actions: filling a glass pot with cold water; pouring the water into a reservoir; placing some filter paper inside a plastic basket; scooping some brown powder into the filter paper; and flipping a switch to turn on the coffee maker. Of course, the details of the procedure vary from household to household. Some people use a metal or reusable filter instead of a paper filter. Others buy whole coffee beans and grind the beans themselves. Some buy more expensive "pod" machines that dispense single servings of coffee. Whatever the detailed procedure might have been, soon the coffee maker begins to gurgle, a little steam escapes, and the wonderful fragrance of coffee fills the whole kitchen. Eventually, they pour some of the black liquid into a cup.

As they sit down to enjoy their first sip of coffee, however, very few of these people realize that they just completed the final steps of a very elegant process in chemical engineering.

Huh? Chemical Engineering?

Wait a second, you might object – what does making a cup of coffee have to do with chemical engineering? Don't chemical engineers make complicated chemicals? Or engineer chemical reactions? How could something as customary as making a cup of coffee count as engineering anything?

Before deciding whether something "counts" as chemical engineering, we should first answer the question: what is chemical engineering? It's worth emphasizing that most people have only a vague idea of what chemical engineers actually do, especially as compared to other engineering professions. Computer engineers design computers. Civil engineers design buildings and bridges. Mechanical engineers design motors and things that move. Biomedical engineers design medical implants and devices. Electrical engineers design electrical circuits. Aerospace engineers design things that go into outer space. All of these engineering professions have well defined subject matters that are readily grasped in the public mind, even if the details are complicated.

In contrast, students of chemical engineering often struggle to convey what a chemical engineer actually does. As the name implies, chemical engineers indeed often work on chemistry and chemical reactions – but that by itself is not the whole story. If the work solely involved chemical reactions, how would a chemical engineer be any different from a chemist? By definition, chemists work on chemistry and chemical reactions, so why is there a whole separate profession known as "chemical engineering"?

Some people might claim, "Oh, chemical engineers work at petroleum refineries to make gasoline." These folks would only be partially correct. Many chemical engineers traditionally have worked in refineries, where crude oil is converted into gasoline and many other products. Further, one can trace the early history of chemical engineering through the development of the petrochemical industry in the late 1800s and early 1900s. In modern times, however, only a fraction of chemical engineers (~20%) actually work in petroleum related fields. On top of that, even within the modern petroleum industry you find many talented chemists; are they doing something different than their chemical engineer colleagues?

The Definition of Chemical Engineering

The answer is most definitely yes: chemical engineers are trained to think in a very different way than chemists or other types of engineers. So, what is chemical engineering? The broadest and simplest definition goes like this:

Chemical engineers design ways to convert matter to a more useful form.

This definition is deceptively simple. Note that no specific product or application is mentioned, nor is there even a specific requirement to include something about chemical reactions. Instead, we have only the incredibly broad criterion that we 'convert' matter to something more 'useful.'

What exactly does this mean? Because there are many kinds of matter, and because there are even more kinds of things that human beings consider 'useful,' there is essentially an infinite number of examples of chemical engineering processes. The classic example, for historical reasons, is that of petroleum. Here we take matter in one form, crude oil which has been extracted from underground, and turn it into a bunch of more useful products: gasoline, fertilizers, plastics, and many others.

However, the starting matter doesn't have to be crude oil, or even a liquid. A second great example involves silicon based computer chips. Here we take silicon (a solid material), and convert it into the chips that run a variety of products, like computers, cell phones and modern TVs. Again, some readers might object, saying "Hold on, computer chips are made by computer engineers, not chemical engineers!" It's absolutely true that computer engineers design the layout of the circuits within a chip – but it's often a chemical engineer that designs the overall process of converting the raw material of silicon into the finished product. Andy Grove, one of the founders of Intel Corporation (arguably the world's largest and most influential producer of computer chips) was trained as a chemical engineer. Likewise, Jack Welch, the long-time CEO of General Electric (one of the world's largest manufacturers of electrical equipment) was also trained as a chemical engineer. Today the computer and semiconductor industries continue to employ a sizable fraction of all chemical engineers (~5%).

A third example of chemical engineering involves a favorite beverage of many college students: beer! Here, just four raw ingredients (barley, hops, yeast and water) are combined and converted into an extremely popular beverage. Unlike the previous two examples, making beer also involves some biology (specifically, the fermentation of sugars into ethanol performed by the yeast), but chemical engineers often design and oversee that process as well. In fact, chemical engineers are heavily recruited not only by brewers (e.g., Anheuser-Busch or Coors), but also by wineries (think Napa Valley) and distillers (think Jack Daniels whiskey or Absolut vodka). Likewise, there are many other examples of modern chemical engineering, including pharmaceutical production, biotechnology, food and agricultural products, equipment design and construction, environmental health and safety, and many others.

OK, but what about coffee?

It should be clear by now that the process of making coffee absolutely counts as an example of chemical engineering. Here we start with the berries of a certain type of evergreen tree or shrub, *Coffea arabica*, which grows well in tropical regions, especially at high altitudes. These bright red (or yellow) berries contain green seeds that are processed, roasted, ground into a powder, and then mixed with hot water to produce the drink we know as coffee. (Note that coffee beans are technically seeds and have nothing to do ˫ everybody calls them beans anyway.) In other words, we take matter in on coffee beans – and we convert it to a much more useful form – coffee that we

Indeed, based on how popular it is, coffee is clearly considered extreme fee in its various forms (e.g., drip-brewed, instant, espresso, etc.) is one of tl consumed beverages in the world. In the United States alone, coffee is a $30 business; Americans consume about 400 *million* cups per *day*!

A key reason for coffee's popularity is the stimulating effect of caffeine, which the seeds of *Coffea arabica* (and other types of coffee trees) have in great abundance. Most of this caffeine stays in the beans during roasting, and then is extracted from the ground beans into the water during the brewing. As a person drinks the coffee, the caffeine enters his or her bloodstream through the lining of the mouth, throat, and stomach and ultimately interacts with the central nervous system to produce a whole range of positive effects: increased wakefulness, clearer flow of thought, better focus, and overall better body coordination. Less well known is that coffee can be prepared so that it tastes *sweet*, without adding any sugar. Coffee aficionados are constantly striving to roast and brew coffee that highlights the sweetness and more delicate flavors of high quality coffees.

The key point here is that all of those millions of people preparing coffee each morning are, whether they know it or not, performing a chemical engineering operation. The drip coffee maker in a person's kitchen might be much smaller than a petroleum refinery, but the underlying principle – of performing some process to convert matter to a more useful form – is exactly the same.

But what makes someone a chemical engineer?

Of course, even though those millions of people making coffee are performing a chemical engineering operation, few of those people would characterize themselves as "chemical engineers." And with good reason: most people making coffee are simply following a protocol that they learned from somebody else.

Note that according to our definition, chemical engineers are individuals who design ways to convert matter to more useful form. There is a lot of meaning packed into that one little word, "design." By "design", we mean that chemical engineers are the ones who plan, simulate, create, and test different procedures for converting some type of matter to a desired more useful form.

The earliest chemical engineers did this design process by trial and error. There is evidence that beer was first brewed in the Neolithic era, more than 10,000 years ago; presumably somebody noticed that if their barley got sufficiently wet, it fermented into something that was intoxicating. Coffee is a more recent invention, probably first made in Ethiopia or Arabia sometime in the 1500s. The coffee beans had to first be roasted and then boiled in water; since chemistry and engineering as disciplines did not develop until much later, presumably the first coffee was likewise developed by a process of trial and error.

Modern chemical engineers often work for companies that are either producing very expensive products (like cell phones), or are producing large quantities of commodity products (like beer), or are designing entirely new processes to make new products (like biofuels). These engineers cannot afford to do things by random trial and error. Instead, they must understand the underlying scientific principles affecting choices in their design, and make decisions about them in a rational manner.

In thinking about coffee, we start to see what differentiates a chemist from a chemical engineer. Typically, chemists focus on just one specific part of the process of converting matter from one form to another: the chemical reaction. Many of the chemical reactions of

...erest in coffee take place during the roasting. This is when the proteins, sugars and acids originally present in the green coffee beans are converted into other types of chemicals that humans perceive as tasting good. As we explore in Lab 3, even more chemical reactions take place during and after brewing (as evidenced by a sizable change in the pH of the coffee with time). A good chemist can measure how fast those chemical reactions take place and characterize the underlying chemical reactions that govern how the various molecules react and transform.

Anybody who has made coffee, however, knows that you need to do more than just roast the beans. That's exactly where chemical engineers enter the picture. Oftentimes in the process of converting matter a chemical reaction is only the first step, and many other steps are required to get the desired "useful form." Anything beyond the chemical reaction – even the design of the reactor vessel in which the reaction occurs – is where chemical engineers come in. Chemical engineers not only have to understand the chemistry, but then they must understand many additional concepts in order to yield a final desired product. Specifically, in the context of coffee, the chemical engineer will design the process with the following questions in mind: How long should I roast the beans? How big of a roaster can I use? How much heat should I deliver to the beans, and what form of energy should I use? After they're roasted, how small should I grind the beans? What temperature water should I use to brew the coffee? How should I deliver the water to the grind, and how fast should I pump it through? What type of filtration should I use – and how does the filter affect the taste of the end product? How do I keep the coffee hot until we're ready to drink it? And by the way, how much is it all going to cost?

The answers to these questions might seem self-evident to you, probably because you've seen how coffee is traditionally made in a drip coffee brewer and you know how much a cappuccino costs at Starbucks. But close your eyes for a moment, and imagine that you've never actually seen how coffee is made. Let's focus on one specific question: how small should I grind the beans? Of course, you can do the trial-and-error approach, and just try a bunch of different sizes until you get something acceptable. The chemical engineer approach, however, is to understand how the size of the grind affects the rate at which the desired chemicals (e.g., the caffeine and the chemicals that taste good) move from inside the solid coffee particles into the liquid water. This process is generally referred to by chemical engineers as "mass transfer," which is just a fancy expression meaning "chemicals move from over here to over there." As we explore in Lab 5, it turns out that the size of the solid particles tremendously affects the rate at which the chemicals move to the liquid – and chemical engineers need to understand how to use this principle to design the overall process in a rational manner.

The Design of Coffee

The laboratory experiences described in this book are intended to serve as a hands-on, non-mathematical introduction to how chemical engineers think, as elucidated by the process of roasting and brewing coffee. The phrase "non-mathematical" is key: the reader needs no prior knowledge of calculus, chemistry, or physics beyond the high school level. The goal is to provide a qualitative overview of key concepts in chemical engineering, so that students get "the big picture," without getting bogged down in complicated calculus or chemistry.

Why coffee? As mentioned above, making coffee is a quintessential operation in chemical engineering. More importantly, unlike the raw materials involved in many other chemical engineering processes (such as petroleum or silicon), green coffee beans are both inexpensive and easy to order online. This means that the reader can personally perform all of the experiments described in this book, and thereby help develop his or her chemical engineering intuition. Even if you think you already know everything there is to know about making coffee, it is unlikely you have approached making coffee the way a trained chemical engineer would. This book will start you down the path of thinking about coffee – and other processes or products – the way a chemical engineer does.

Toward that end, this laboratory guidebook is organized as follows. First, we take care of some essential preliminaries with an overview of all the necessary supplies and equipment for those readers setting up the labs at home. Most importantly, we review key safety aspects and introduce the main concepts of tasting coffee in Lab 0.

The remainder of the book is divided into two distinct parts: analysis and design. Labs 1 through 6 each focus on a core chemical engineering concept, with an emphasis on understanding how to perform "engineering analysis" on each concept. Labs 1 and 2 examine the concept of a "process flow diagram," and how conservation of mass must be satisfied in each step of the process. Lab 3 explores the effect of chemical reactions on how the taste of brewed coffee changes with time, while Lab 4 examines the meaning of "energy" and how it pertains to roasting and brewing coffee. The concepts of "flux" and "mass transfer" are then illustrated in Lab 5 with experiments on the effect of grind size, extraction time, and water temperature on the strength of the brew. Lab 6 introduces key concepts of fluid motion and "colloid science," and explores their ramifications on the filtration of coffee. At the end of each lab we also include a "bonus question" that highlights key aspects of the lab topic as they pertain to the process of making coffee.

In the second part, we then shift gears from "analysis" to "design." Labs 7 and 8 guide the students in first optimizing and then scaling up their own unique process for roasting and brewing. Finally, everything culminates in Lab 9, which is where students compete in the engineering design challenge: to make the best tasting coffee (as judged by a blind taste panel) using the least amount of energy. It is difficult to make good tasting coffee – but it is even more difficult to make good tasting coffee while using little energy!

As emphasized in this introduction, the main point of The Design of Coffee is to teach students how to think like an engineer. Nonetheless, even if you decide your interests lie outside of engineering, you definitely will understand on a deeper level how to make a truly excellent cup of coffee – a useful skill no matter what you choose to do in life!

Supplies & Equipment – What Do We Need?

If you are reading this book as part of a course offered at a school or a workshop, then you don't need to worry about this section. The instructor will already have gathered all of the necessary equipment and supplies that you will need to perform the upcoming labs. Unless you are curious, you can skip this section and move on to Lab 0 to review very important safety considerations and begin learning about tasting coffee.

If, however, you are setting up the labs to do on your own, then you need to give some thought and attention to procuring all of the necessary supplies and equipment. The goal of this section is to help interested individuals identify what they need to borrow or purchase.

Before getting into the details, a couple comments are necessary. First, all of the specific items listed here have been found by us to be useful for the purpose of learning about the science and engineering of coffee. There are many great brewing and roasting vendors, and their inclusion or exclusion on this list should not be construed as a recommendation either for or against them in terms of their quality. The items listed here were chosen with an eye toward elucidating key principles inexpensively – not for making the "best" coffee.

Second, we strongly recommend that individual readers team up with other interested people to do the labs. One reason for this is practical: it's easier to split up some of the work while doing the labs, and it's kind of silly to hold a design contest (Lab 9) if there is only one coffee to taste! But another reason is philosophical: in industry, engineers almost invariably work on teams, and indeed most engineering schools emphasize teamwork and group activities in their curricula. We recommend that you find a few other friends interested in coffee to do the experiments collaboratively, and to do the coffee design contest competitively. We think you'll find that it's also much more fun!

Items marked below with an asterisk are used in every lab, and so won't be listed under the necessary equipment for each lab overview – you will still need them even though they are not specifically listed there. Items needed in Labs 7 to 9 are only potentially needed because of the open-ended nature of those labs.

Coffee beans

☐ Roasted coffee beans, about 1 pound (Labs 1 – 3)

☐ Green coffee beans, about 10 pounds, at least two varieties (Labs 2 – 8)

Roasted coffee beans are available at basically every grocery store and cafe. Green coffee beans are less expensive but need to be specially ordered. An online vendor we like is Sweet Maria's, or their wholesale branch (Coffee Shrub) for larger purchases. How many green beans you use will depend on the time spent in the design trials (Labs 7 & 8).

Grinder

☐ Baratza Encore grinder * (Labs 1 – 9)

Coffee aficionados swear by the more expensive cone-and-burr grinders, but we find that a standard $20 electric blade grinder (like the Krups F203) is sufficient for the labs described here. If you do use a standard electric blade grinder, gently shake the grinder up and down while it's grinding to help make sure the beans are evenly grinded.

Roasters
- ☐ Nesco Professional Home Coffee Roaster (Labs 2 – 8)
- ☐ West Bend Air Crazy Hot Air Popcorn Popper (Labs 4, 7 – 8)

These are both small "table-top" roasters, perfect for the small batches we'll be making here. The Nesco is specifically designed for coffee and is a bit more expensive (about $150). The popcorn roaster is much less expensive ($20) but works great on coffee. If cost is an issue, you can do almost all the roasting described here just with the popcorn roaster. Note that the popcorn popper must have air vents designed to swirl the air (either clockwise or counter-clockwise when looking into it). Don't buy one with a mesh that blows the hot air straight up, the beans won't rotate and they'll eventually catch on fire.

Brewing
- ☐ Mr. Coffee Coffee Brewer, 4-cup (TGF-4) (Labs 1–3, 7–9)
- ☐ Clever Coffee Dripper, large (Labs 3 – 9)
- ☐ AeroPress Coffee Maker (Labs 6 – 9)
- ☐ Bodum 4-cup French Press (Labs 6 – 9)
- ☐ Bonavita 1.0 L variable Temp Gooseneck Electric Kettle (Labs 3 – 9)

The Mr. Coffee is a standard drip brewer that has a built in water heater. Any simple brewer can be used – but you will be taking it apart and reassembling it. The other three brewers (Clever Coffee, AeroPress, and French Press) require an external source of hot water. We find the Bonavita electric kettle to be convenient since it has a built-in thermostat.

Filters
- ☐ Appropriate size filter papers for various brewers * (Labs 1 – 9)
- ☐ Able brewing DISK filter (metallic) for AeroPress (Labs 6– 9)

Make sure you get the right filter paper for each of your brewers; Lab 6 requires a metal filter for the AeroPress to compare paper and metal filtration. (It makes a difference!)

Glassware and Storage
- ☐ Large glass mug or measuring cup (Labs 4 – 9)
- ☐ Bormioli Rocco Easy Bar Espresso Cups, Clear, 3.5 oz * (Labs 1 – 9)
- ☐ Glass graduated cylinder (500 mL) (Lab 2)
- ☐ Small paper cups (Labs 3, 5)
- ☐ Large & small mixing bowls (Labs 2 – 8)
- ☐ ¼ lb Clear Valve Coffee Bags (Labs 2 – 8)
- ☐ Zojirushi HandyPot - Glass Lined Stainless Steel 1L (Lab 9)

Transparent glass mugs are preferred because they allow you to see the coffee. You only need big ones for some of the brewing methods; the small espresso mugs are perfect for tasting. Small paper cups are useful for several of the time sensitive measurements (e.g., pH or TDS versus time) because you can write the sample time on the side. The graduated cylinder is great for measuring the volume change of the beans upon roasting. A large bowl is useful for catching chaff from the popcorn roaster, while small bowls are useful for measuring

Supplies & Equipment

masses. The Clear Valve bags are super convenient for storing roasted beans, since they're designed to allow carbon dioxide to off-gas (without over-pressurizing a container). Allow beans to cool to room temperature before you put them in the plastic bag! The Zojirushi carafe keeps up to 1 liter of coffee warm and is perfect for the blind taste test.

Analytical Measurements

- ☐ Digital kitchen scale with 0.1 gram resolution* (Labs 1 – 9)
- ☐ Digital thermometer and thermocouple, 6" and 12" (Labs 1, 3, 4)
- ☐ Ecotestr pH-2 Handheld pH meter (Lab 3)
- ☐ P4400 Kill-A-Watt Electricity Usage Meter (Labs 3 – 9)
- ☐ VST Coffee Lab III Digital Refractometer (Labs 5 – 8)

The digital scale is absolutely essential since you will be weighing things many times in every lab; brands like Hario or Acaia are good because they have a built-in timer useful for monitoring extraction time. The digital thermometer is convenient, but in a pinch you could you use a regular (spirit-filled) thermometer. The pH meter is primarily used in Lab 3, so if cost is an issue you could skip it or try using paper pH strips. The Kill-a-Watt electricity meter is indispensable since our main engineering goal is to minimize the energy usage, but fortunately it's only about $20. Finally, the most expensive item by far is the coffee refractometer (which tells you the total dissolved solids, or "strength," of your coffee). It costs about $750. This is a crucial measurement, though, so if you're serious about coffee (and can afford it) you'll get one. If cost is an issue, however, you could buy a hand-held conductivity meter (about $20) to estimate the TDS. It's much cheaper, but also far less accurate.

Miscellaneous

- ☐ Screwdriver (Lab 1)
- ☐ Metal mesh colander (Labs 2 – 8)
- ☐ Pastry brush (Labs 2 – 8)
- ☐ Silicone mitts (Labs 1 – 9)
- ☐ Simple Microscope (Labs 6)

The metal mesh colander is great for quickly cooling your beans after the roast, and the pastry brush is helpful for cleaning chaff out of the roasters. The mitts are for handling hot items. If you have access to a simple optical or USB microscope, then you can observe the effects of filtration on the coffee colloids in Lab 6. A microscope with 400x total magnification and phase contrast is nice but not necessary.

Finally, you'll need access to a sink, electricity, and a few feet of table space. Modern electrical codes require electrical outlets near sinks to have GFCI protection, and it's a good idea that your outlets have that (in case you drop an electrical apparatus in the sink). The room should have at least standard ventilation (don't roast in an enclosed or unventilated space). A dishwasher is convenient but not necessary.

In terms of time commitment, each lab is designed to take about 2 hours, including clean up. Although you can combine multiple labs in one day, it's better to space them out by at least one or two days. This gives roasted beans time to off-gas and develop their full flavor, and gives you time to absorb the lessons learned in previous labs.

Lab 0 – Safety Overview and Introduction to Tasting

Objectives: In this preliminary lab we will first review important safety issues associated with hot coffee in the laboratory. We will then perform a traditional "cupping" to get experience with the taste of high quality brewed coffee. The goal is for you to learn the key sensory attributes that you will use to judge your coffee.

Equipment:

☐ Fresh roasted coffee   ☐ Hot water   ☐ Official cupping cups   ☐ Spoon

Lab Activities:

☐ Part A – safety review

☐ Part B – traditional cupping of at least two different coffees

Report:

☐ Signed safety sheet

Background – Safety

Before you step foot in lab, the first crucial activity is for you to review the safety rules and expectations for the coffee lab. Your pre-lab assignment for Lab 0 is straightforward: simply read the safety rules and laboratory orientation, then sign the written safety sheet at the bottom of the next page. Submit the signed safety sheet, either as an image (e.g., a cell phone photo) or a PDF scan. You don't need to submit this page; the pictorial overview is intended only to reinforce the written material on the safety sheet. If you have any questions about safety or procedure at any time, do not hesitate to ask your teaching assistant and/or instructor, or your colleagues or friends if performing experiments at home. Better safe than sorry!

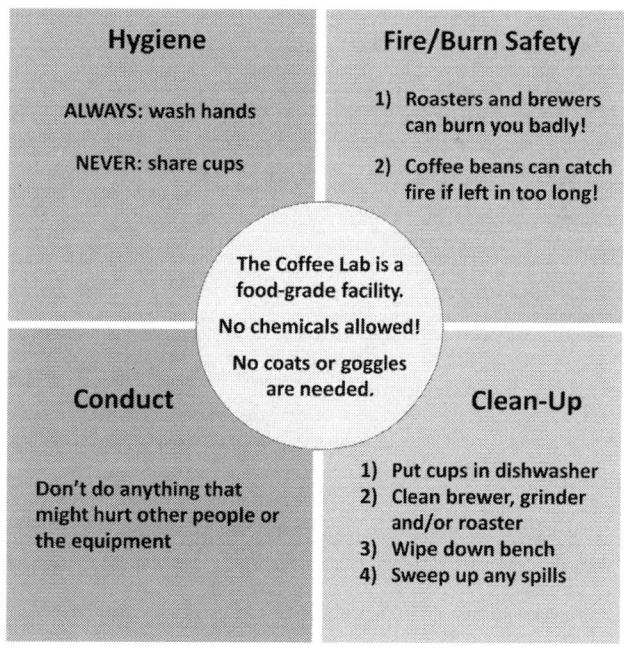

Because this is a preliminary lab, you don't need to write a formal lab report (for either Part A or Part B). If you are part of a class then you simply need to sign and submit the safety sheet; if you are at home, then make sure you understand the safety aspects described here.

Safety Orientation for "The Coffee Lab"

1) **Food grade facility.** The "coffee lab" is a food grade facility. Unlike many laboratories, you may eat and drink food. This means, however, that absolutely NO HAZARDOUS CHEMICALS / MATERIALS are allowed inside the coffee lab. Do not bring any chemicals inside the lab.

2) **No lab coats or goggles.** Since there are no chemicals, you do **not** need a lab coat, lab gloves, or eye protection. Regular clothing and shoes are fine.

3) **Hygiene – washing hands.** You must wash your hands with soap and water upon entering the lab. Likewise, wash your hands after you use the restroom; after coughing, sneezing, or blowing your nose; or after doing anything else that soils your hands.

4) **Hygiene – no sharing cups.** Do not share cups with anybody else. Use sticky labels to identify your personal cup at the beginning of each lab session. Avoid the temptation to take "just a small sip" from somebody else's cup. If you think your cup is dirty or was accidentally shared, get a new one.

5) **Burn safety.** The main safety hazard with coffee is the risk of burns. The coffee pots and roasters can get hot enough to cause severe burns if contacted with bare skin. Exercise great caution around them; only handle the brewers and roasters by their designated handles. **Always pour hot coffee into a cup placed on the lab bench, never into a cup in somebody's hand.** If you do receive a burn, immediately begin running cool water over it in the sink and notify your teaching assistant and/or instructor.

6) **Fire safety.** Just like bread can catch fire in a toaster, coffee beans can catch fire in a roaster. Never leave your roaster unattended. If it begins to smoke heavily, turn it off immediately. If the beans stop moving, turn it off immediately. If the beans do catch on fire, turn off the roaster and, if feasible, place a 'fire blanket' over the roaster to smother the flames. Notify the teaching assistant and/or instructor of any observed open flames, no matter how insignificant they might seem. Pay special attention on safe use of all roasters. Note the location of the room exits, the first aid kit, and the fire extinguisher.

7) **No horseplay or misconduct.** Any individual who purposely engages in unsafe behavior will be expelled from the lab and likely fail the course. Examples of misconduct include: throwing things, horseplay, (wrestling, pushing, tickling, etc.), or putting anything other than coffee beans into a roaster or brewer.

8) **No unapproved equipment.** No personal brewing or roasting equipment may be brought from home into the lab. Absolutely no open flames are allowed in the lab (no camp stoves, candles, etc.)

9) **End of lab cleanup (MANDATORY).** At the end of each lab session, your group must clean your station. Place all coffee cups in the dishwasher, and wash all brewing glassware you used with soap and water. Spray and wipe down your area of lab bench, and use a hand-broom to sweep up any coffee grounds or beans you might have spilled on the ground. IMPORTANT: Before you leave, confirm with your teaching assistant and/or instructor that your lab cleanup is adequate to receive full points.

I affirm that I carefully read and understand the expectations for conduct and safety in the Coffee Lab.

Signature: _____ Date: _____

Print name: _____

Student ID Number: _____ Section number: _____

Background – Tasting

Coffee tasting is challenging. Experts spend years developing their palate to identify subtle differences in each cup. Here we provide just the basic definitions of the main sensory attributes that we will use to judge coffees in our blind taste tests.

When tasting, first smell the coffee, then loudly **slurp** some in your mouth. By slurping, you create smaller droplets (aerosols), which accomplish two goals. First, they help coat all of your taste buds throughout your mouth, so that your entire palate is involved in the evaluation. Second, the smaller droplets have a higher surface area-to-volume ratio, which accelerates volatilization of the aroma molecules that travel up your "retro-nasal" passage way. (A great deal of "taste" is actually "smell"!) Some tasters find it helpful to "chew" the coffee in their mouth to make sure everything is maximally distributed. Finally, after you swallow, continue to assess the aftertaste. The main scoring categories are defined as follows.

Fragrance The aromatic aspects of the coffee, as detected by an initial smell before tasting in the mouth. A better fragrance receives a higher score.

Flavor The coffee's taste character, in between the first impressions given by the first aroma and acidity to its final taste (also known as the "mid-range" notes). It is the combined impression of all the taste bud sensations and retro-nasal aromas that go from mouth to nose.

Aftertaste The length or duration of positive flavor (both taste and aroma) emanating from the back of the palate and remaining after the coffee is swallowed. If the aftertaste is either short or unpleasant, a lower score should be given.

Acidity Often described as "bright" when favorable, "sour" when unpleasant, or "dull" or "flat" when missing. Compare to Italian salad dressing: you want an appropriate amount of acidity from the vinegar, but too much vinegar makes it unpleasantly sour. Acidity contributes to the liveliness, sweetness, and fresh-fruit character, especially when the coffee is first slurped. A lack of acidity (a "dullness" or "flatness") receives a low score, but too much acidity ("sourness") also receives a low score. Give a high score to a "bright", lively acidity that enhances the coffee flavor.

Body The tactile feeling of the coffee liquid in the mouth, highly related to the "viscosity" of the liquid. The presence of colloids and sucrose in the coffee contribute to higher body. A "watery" coffee can have good flavor but lack body, while a "thick" coffee can have strong body but bad flavor. Give high scores for pleasant body.

Balance The overall impression of the coffee. Ideally a coffee is balanced between all of the above attributes, with none dominating over any other. Think of this category as a subjective "fudge factor"… if smelling and tasting the coffee overall was a positive experience, give it a high balance score. If, on the other hand, you overall had a negative experience, then give it a negative score.

Sweetness How sweet is the coffee? When we talk about sweetness, we don't mean to add sugar to the cup! Perhaps surprisingly, certain coffees can be perceived as having a sweetness due to the presence of sugars and some complex carbohydrates. Black coffee is never as sweet as soda (which has a huge amount of added sugar!), but high quality coffees have a pronounced sweetness that is highly prized.

Defects Defects are off flavors that detract from the taste. For example, a recent problem with some Rwandan coffees is known as the potato defect. As its name suggests, the potato defect results in the aroma of freshly-peeled potatoes, which is not what you want in a quality coffee.

Many coffee experts advocate a pretty straightforward way to approach tasting coffee, perhaps best summarized by Nick Cho (founder of Wrecking Ball Coffee in San Francisco): "The four steps to critical coffee tasting, in order, are sweetness, negatives, acidity, and flavor notes." Nick emphasizes that having a naturally sweet tasting cup of coffee is the most important feature or attribute (no added sugar!), next is avoiding negatives in the flavors or qualities, followed by good acidity or brightness, and finally those flavor notes from differentiate great tasting coffee including coffee varietals. Together, these attributes can culminate in "nirvana in a cup" - distinguishing a truly great cup of coffee from average.

Part A – Safety Review

First, before beginning any experiments, review again the "Lab and Safety" orientation one more time. Although we're "simply making coffee," there are nonetheless important safety issues regarding health, burns, and fire. Make sure you know where a fire blanket and first aid kit are located, in the remote chance that an accident occurs and you do need them. Also make sure you understand what is expected in terms of cleanup after you are done.

Part B – Cupping Coffee Like a Professional

Time to brew and taste some awesome coffee! For this preliminary laboratory experiment, we will follow the professional cupping guidelines developed by the Specialty Coffee Association of America (SCAA). These guidelines might seem unusual to you, because traditionally the coffee is tasted without any filtration: you simply dump hot water into a cup with some grounds, and then taste directly out of that cup! The details, however, are highly specific, so let's get into them.

First, you should ideally have freshly roasted coffee with a light to light-medium roast. According to the SCAA the beans should have been roasted within the last 24 hours with a minimum of 8 hours of resting time after roasting. Quality coffees can be brewed with beans roasted up to 2 weeks prior, but part of professionally cupping is to determine what beans you should buy – so the beans are frequently roasted the day before the cupping.

Take the opportunity to compare the aroma of the roasted beans to the aroma of the green (unroasted) beans… the difference is remarkable! Can you detect a difference in aroma of the green beans of two different origins?

Cupping Procedure (Tasting Like a Professional)

1. Measure about 10 grams of beans for each individual who will be cupping.
2. Grind the coffee, medium coarse (about 20 on a Baratza Encore).
3. Carefully add about 8.25 grams of ground coffee into each cup and cover the cup with the plastic cover. Repeat for each type of coffee.
4. Add enough water to the water kettle for about 155 grams of water per cup and heat to 93°C. (So, for 3 people and 2 cups each, heat at least 930 grams.)
5. Evaluate the aromas of the dry ground coffees and record your impressions into your cupping data sheet.
6. Once the water is 93°C, carefully add 150 grams of water to the cup, making sure to fully wet the ground coffee. Start your timer.
7. After 3 to 5 minutes, break the crust at the top of the cup by stirring your spoon around 3 times. Smell the foam and liquid on the spoon and record your wet coffee aroma impressions.
8. After 8 to 10 minutes, start to taste (or slurp) the coffee with the spoon and evaluate the flavor (score from 1 to 10, with 10 being the best), aftertaste (1 to 10), acidity (1 to 10), body (1 to 10), and balance (−10 to 5).

The cups themselves have specific requirements (don't just use any old mugs you have lying around). The cups should be made out of either white ceramic or tempered glass, and they should hold about 8 fluid ounces (near 250 mL), with a top diameter of about 3 to 3.5 inches. All of the cups that you taste out of should be identical, since your perceptions can be affected by the shape, color, or feel of the cup.

Note that the beans must *not* be ground in advance. In fact, the closer the grinding is to brewing the better. The wonderful aromas of freshly ground coffee that you smell mean that you are losing those volatile components to the air, and we want to capture as much as possible in the brew. The recommended size is just slightly coarser than you would typically use in an automatic drip coffee – a setting of about 20 on a Baratza grinder.

After grinding place 8.25 grams of ground coffee into your cup. Cover the cup with a lid and set up a second cup in an identical manner with the other coffee you will be tasting. Cover that cup and start heating fresh water to 93°C. While the water is heating remove the covers and smell the aromas of the freshly ground coffees. Record your impressions of the aromas in the Data sheet on the next page. The coffee flavor wheel can help you identify aromas, beyond simply saying "it smells like coffee." For example, some coffees are known for berry or fruit aromas while others have a hint of chocolate or nuts.

Once the water is 93°C, carefully pour 150 grams of water into your cup. Make sure you fully wet the ground coffee. Set your timer and allow the cup to sit undisturbed for at least 3 but no more than 5 minutes. Break the crust of ground coffee at the top of your cup and again smell the aromas. There's even an official way to break the crust – stir three times and pull the spoon from the cup – while the foam and liquid is running down the back of the spoon (into your cup, not onto the floor or table). Smell and record your impressions of aromas. The aromas of the dry and wet grounds comprise the fragrance portion of the score.

After the grounds have been allowed to steep for 8 – 10 minutes you can start tasting (or slurping!) the brew. While the coffee is hot, your initial impressions should focus on the flavor and aftertaste. As it starts to cool, turn your attention to the acidity and the body. Next, score the balance, mouth feel, and sweetness. Continue to taste and adjust your evaluations and scores as your perception of the flavors and qualities change with temperature.

Cupping Data Sheet

Coffee type_____

Aroma Evaluations of ground and wet coffee:
_____
_____

Sensory Evaluations:

Flavor: _____
_____

Aftertaste: _____ Acidity: _____

Body: _____ Balance: _____

Comments (Sweetness, Defects, Other): _____
_____ Total Score_____

Coffee type_____

Aroma Evaluations of ground and wet coffee:
_____
_____

Sensory Evaluations:

Flavor: _____
_____

Aftertaste: _____ Acidity: _____

Body: _____ Balance: _____

Comments (Sweetness, Defects, Other): _____
_____ Total Score_____

Lab 0 Bonus Box – Why Do Coffees Taste Different?

Now that you've seen and smelled some green and roasted coffee beans, we should discuss a key point: coffee is a highly variable biological material! Much like the grapes used to make fine wines, coffee beans vary tremendously in taste depending on where they are grown and with how much care they are picked and processed. High quality, specialty coffee is mainly produced in tropical, equatorial zones at elevations greater than 3000 feet. Coffee "beans" are the seeds of the fruit (coffee cherry) of the *Coffea* shrub or tree. A mature plant typically produces about 20-60 pounds of coffee cherries each year, yielding between 3 and 9 pounds of green coffee beans. To maximize the quality of the green beans, the cherries must be harvested at their peak ripeness – typically bright red, yellow, or orange in color depending on the variety. Because the cherries ripen at different rates, harvesting of optimally ripe coffee cherries is a very labor intensive endeavor with multiple picks.

Workers on a coffee plantation (typically in a less affluent tropical country) had to care for the coffee trees, pick the red cherries, de-pulp the cherries to remove the fruity flesh, wash and dry the beans, sort out the bad beans by hand, bag the good beans, and then transport them to the nearest buyer – oftentimes by mule down the side of a mountain. In a sense, by the time the consumer or the commercial roaster receives a shipment of green coffee beans, most of the hard work has already been done.

There are fascinating scientific aspects to the processing of coffee cherries to usable green beans, which is done primarily through two main processing methods: wet or dry processing. Ultimately, the goal of processing is to separate the beans from the fruit and reduce their moisture content to 10-13%. This enables transport and storage of the green beans for up to one year with little degradation, making it easy to ship the beans all over the world.

In dry processing the growers lay the coffee cherries out in the sun to dry. Over the course of 3 to 4 weeks the cherries are raked and rotated every few hours and protected from moisture to ensure even drying without mildew or spoilage. In some cases mechanical dryers are used after a few days to accelerate the drying process. Once the cherries are dried sufficiently, the outer hull is removed to release the coffee beans. Dry processing is used in production areas with limited access to water and is more variable due to the reliance on climate conditions during the drying process. On the other hand, wet processing uses a hand or mechanical depulper to remove the outer skin and some of the pulp from the cherries, and then a lot of water to ultimately separate the seeds from the fruit. As there is still some pulp on the seeds after depulping, they are stored for a few hours to a couple of days and allowed to "ferment" a bit to breakdown the plant cell walls (cellulose) and enable the residual pulp/mucilage to be removed from the seed more easily by washing. Fermentation is also going on during dry processing, but is not controlled by washing steps.

The word "fermentation" refers to a biological process in which yeast or bacteria convert sugars into different chemicals (such as the alcohol in beer). Moreover, it has long been held that a crucial step in the final flavor and aroma profile of roasted coffee is the fermentation step during the processing of the coffee cherries, as the coffee beans produced via the different methods yield notably different taste profiles. Some growers and coffee processors are experimenting with various yeasts (think beer brewing) to try to enhance the flavor characteristics by better controlling the fermentation portion of the process. The impact of these experiments is still up in the air, but in the future you might have an IPA or Ale yeast fermented green bean. More recently, variations in the partial germination of the coffee beans (recall the "beans" are really seeds) during wet vs. dry processing steps are being studied more closely as germination may be just as, or even more, important to the final flavors. The word "germination" refers to the process by which a seed yields a plant. Given that coffee bean processing has evolved through a trial and error process - limited or impacted by the local environment (humidity and temperature), availability of water, equipment, time and resources – we hope that an even better understanding of how to produce great coffee will be available in the near future.

The key point is that both a huge amount of manual labor and a great deal of biological activity go into the preparation of green coffee beans. Despite all this hard work and the interesting scientific aspects, for the purpose of this book we focus on what happens to green coffee beans after all this processing. In other words, we treat green coffee beans as our starting material. There is nothing unusual about this; many other chemical engineering processes involve "raw" starting materials that were actually pre-processed in some way. Moreover, from a practical perspective, in the United States at least it is difficult to obtain unprocessed coffee cherries.

An important point, however, must be emphasized: because coffee is a biological material, it is subject to tremendous variability. Green coffee beans vary wildly in their composition depending on what region they're grown. Beans grown in Brazil are quite distinct from those grown in Indonesia, Ethiopia or anywhere else. Even beans from ostensibly identical coffee plants in the same plantation can also differ, depending on soil characteristics, how wet or dry the local microclimate is, even the precise altitude of the coffee plant. (Recall many coffee plants are grown in mountainous terrain.) Moreover, the coffee cherry processing method will alter otherwise similar green coffee beans into dramatically different beans.

All of these factors will influence the taste of the final brewed coffee! Perhaps surprisingly, black coffee can have amazing flavors, including berry, floral, citrus, chocolate, and vanilla. Black coffee can even have a pronounced sweet taste – without adding sugar. To give an idea of the tremendous flavor profiles possible, here is an example review of a particular 2014 coffee from the "Gitesi" cooperative in Rwanda (in south central Africa):

Gitesi continues to produce some of the best coffee we see from [Rwanda], and this year's lots are of significant quality. Right from the get-go, Gitesi [coffee] has such an attractive set of aromatics, perfumed with dried wildflowers, red honey, and clove spice in the dry grounds. Aspects of complex sugar browning come into full view when you add the hot water, with a rich sweetness of caramel candies and vanilla hanging heavy in the air and with a floral note ready to be released on the break. City plus roasts are intensely sweet, flavors of raw cane juice providing the backdrop. Citrus notes pop out on top, lemon oil and orange blossom florals, as well as a candied peel note. There is a flavor of pineapple upside down cake as the coffee cools, candied tropical fruits, and baking spices. Dark roasts are very sweet too and have cinnamon bark punch, with chocolate/cacao roast tones. Gitesi changes quite a bit from light to dark roasts, and the sweetness is potent all the way to the outer edge of Full City (but for the most complex cup, don't stray far from City+/Full City). The finish is very clean, with notes of peach and chocolate syrup filling out the aftertaste.

For contrast, here is a 2015 review of a Guatemalan coffee from the "Finca Rosma" plantation:

> You get a sense of Rosma's sweetness straight from the grinder. The dry fragrance has a smell of caramel-coated raisin and all-spice, a nice butter and sugar sweetness. The wet aroma has the essence of dried fruits with brown sugar, so much caramel and cream through to the break, even a floral touch too. Full City roasts show chocolate roast tones, burned sugar and such, and a nice syrupy-sweet break. Rosma is a coffee that cups with equally high levels of sweetness, fruit, and acidity. From City to Full City, this coffee is loaded with honey and caramel, and the darker you take it, the more high percent cacao bar is expressed. The acidity 'pops' too, all the way to Full City, refreshing like fruit juice. City roasts show hints of apple and white grape, while Full City roasts develop darker fruit notes, plum and concord grape, sweet and juicy. Body is big with this coffee, conveying the fruit and chocolate notes nicely well into the finish. This makes a great brewed coffee in the City to Full City roast ranges. We pulled a shot of espresso with our Full City roast, and it was so delicious - thick, rich chocolate flavors, and deeply sweet.

These reviews were written by Tom Thompson and colleagues at Sweet Maria's, which is one of many retail distributors of specialty green beans. We urge you to do a simple web search "green coffee beans for roasting" to get a sense for the astonishing variety of green beans available for purchase. Many cost only $6 per pound.

Why does one batch of green coffee beans taste different from another? Everything hinges on the unique chemical composition of the green beans. There are more than 1,000 uniquely identified molecules that give rise to the flavors present in coffee, and as mentioned above, minor changes in growing conditions and processing procedure can alter the relative composition. The roasting process can enhance or diminish different aspects of the bean's flavor profile. Moreover, many of the most subtle flavors (such as "pineapple upside down cake" or "floral orange tea") are highly volatile and transient. If you wait too long after roasting, the flavors dissipate… and you're left with the more bitter molecules. Most coffee aficionados recommend that you store roasted coffee in a sealed container and brew it about 2 to 7 days after roasting. You can still brew the coffee after longer delays, but you won't catch the types of refined and varied flavors that are possible (as highlighted in the reviews above).

Of course, there is more to making coffee than simply brewing it within the right time period! The upcoming labs will help you think more scientifically about the process of roasting and brewing coffee, with the ultimate goal of brewing coffee with delightful flavors like those described here.

Part I

Analysis of Coffee

Lab 1 – Reverse Engineering a Drip Coffee Brewer

Objectives: In this lab we will overview and perform the process of brewing drip coffee, and learn about the important "brew ratio." We will partially disassemble a Mr. Coffee brewer to consider how it works from an engineering perspective.

Equipment:

☐ Mr. Coffee ☐ Thermometer and thermocouple ☐ Screwdriver

Activities:

☐ Part A – one brew in the Mr. Coffee, to learn how to brew and to introduce R_{brew}

☐ Part B – partial disassembly of the Mr. Coffee to reverse engineer it

☐ Part C – one more brew with temperature measurements

Report:

☐ Labeled photos of the Mr. Coffee (inside and outside)

☐ Qualitative process flow diagram for brewing

☐ Scatter plot of temperature vs. time

☐ Paragraph discussing key questions about the lab

Background

There are two key components of engineering practice: *analysis* and *design*. Engineering *analysis* is the process of learning how a system of interest works, typically by combining experimental observations with theoretical interpretations. In contrast, engineering *design* refers to using that understanding to create or improve a process to accomplish some specific goal – for example, to make the best tasting coffee using the least amount of energy.

In this lab, we will be performing a specific type of engineering analysis called "reverse engineering," where we take a process that somebody else has already designed and figure out how it works. Specifically, we will reverse engineer a standard drip brewer, with a focus on the question, "What makes the water move?" Furthermore, as part of this process we will make a "process flow diagram." The picture at right shows a simplified and **incomplete** process flow diagram superimposed over a photo of a Mr. Coffee. Your goals in this first lab are to (1) reverse

engineer a Mr. Coffee and (2) make a qualitative process flow diagram for this brewing process. In the next lab you will make a more complete and quantitative process flow diagram that includes roasting.

Background – Reverse Engineering a Drip Brewer

We could just tell you exactly how a drip brewer works, but that would be boring. Instead, we want you to figure it out! To help you along the way, here are some of the items you will discover as you inspect the brewer.

Spring valve – The first thing you should identify before you even open up the brewer. When you push on the spring, the valve opens; when you stop pushing on it, the valve closes.

Power Switch – This is how you turn it on. It's easy to find from the outside; what does it look like from the inside? How do you think it works?

Wires – As soon as you open up the brewer you will definitely see several electrical wires inside. As you examine them, consider these two questions. (i) Why are they coated in plastic? (ii) Why are there two wires connected to the heater? Why couldn't just one wire deliver the electricity to it? (This is a subtle question!) Hint: pretend you're an electron: what path would you follow through the circuitry? On some models, you will have even more wires headed to indicator lights or other features. In a simple 4-cup Mr. Coffee brewer, one set of wires is only used to illuminate the power switch; where does the remainder go?

Heating tube – There will be a large metallic "u"-shaped tube inside. Why do you think it's made out of metal? Why not plastic or ceramic? What else does this heating tube keep hot beside the water inside of it?

Electrical heater – When you make electricity flow through a "resistor," the resistor heats up. This is the same effect you see in an incandescent light bulb, where it heats up so much that it starts glowing.

Thermal Fuse – A thermal fuse is a special type of wire that allows electrical currents to pass through, but if the temperature gets too high, a connection physically melts and breaks, stopping the current. (Why do you think you might want a thermal fuse or two inside a coffee maker?)

Thermostat – Depending on the model of coffee maker, you might have a thermostat that regulates the flow of electricity. If the temperature gets too high, the thermostat simply cuts the electricity to the heater. More expensive brewers may have a "thermistor." A "resistor" resists the flow of electricity, making the current smaller (and thus the temperature smaller). A "thermistor" is a resistor whose resistance depends on temperature. The higher the temperature, the higher the resistance, and the lower the current.

Check valve – This can be difficult to locate! (Look closely inside the plastic tubes that carry the water.) Also known as a "one-way" valve, a check valve only allows fluid to flow through it one direction. Typically there is a flap or ball inside that opens when you push it one way but closes when you push it the other way.

Background – Process Flow Diagrams

As mentioned above, one goal of this lab is for you to construct a "process flow diagram" for the process of making coffee. You can think of a process flow diagram as a kind of map that shows how different materials move through different processes or pieces of equipment. Typically the process flow diagram shows major pieces of equipment and omits minor details (such as piping). A process flow diagram for a large scale operation, such as a petroleum refinery, can be extremely complicated – there can be thousands of pieces of equipment and unit operations.

Here we start simple. Examine the figure below, which shows a simplified process flow diagram for a process you're probably familiar with: doing laundry! Note it includes both the obvious "material streams" that you handle personally (like the clothes) as well as the streams you probably don't think about (like the waste water). Importantly, conservation of mass (discussed in Lab 2) must be satisfied around each unit operation. Check that the mass going into the washer is equal to the mass exiting it. (In fact, can you figure out the mass of dirt on the dirty clothes? It's possible to calculate based on the given information.)

A coffee brewer is much simpler, but still requires thought. The most important thing is to think about "what goes in" and "what goes out" in each material stream. Specifically, there are two obvious streams of material that go into the coffee brewer – cold water and dry coffee grounds – but how many streams come out? There are at least three, and each one needs its own arrow. Keep this question in mind as you perform your first brews!

Example of a Process Flow Diagram: Doing your Laundry!

(Note that every material stream is shown entering or exiting the correct unit operation)

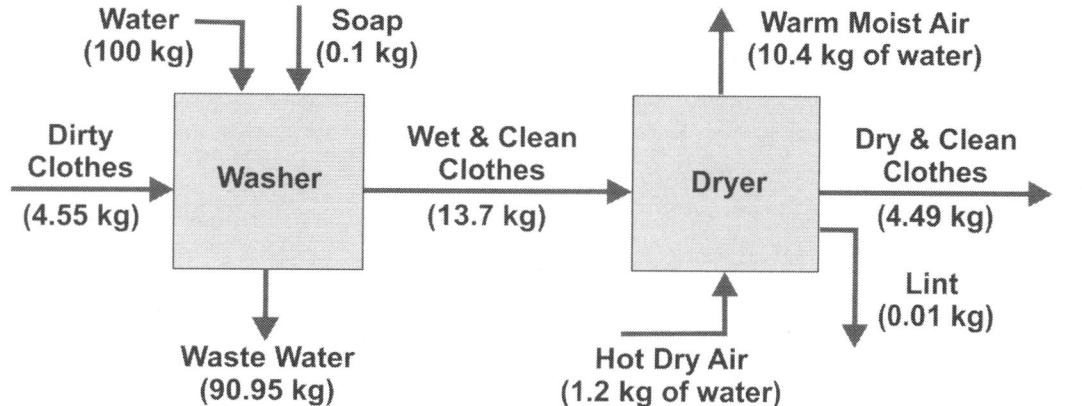

Part A – Your First Drip Brew

Time to brew! First, get some roasted coffee beans (about 20 grams), and place them in the grinder. For a drip brew, you want a "medium" grind, which is not a fine powder, but more like kosher salt or coarse beach sand. (On Baratza Encore grinders this is a grind size setting of about 18.) Place a weighed mass of coffee grounds into the basket. Then pour a known <u>mass</u> (not volume) of cold water into the back of the drip brewer. How much water? The metric that matters is known as the "brew ratio," defined as

$$R_{brew} = \frac{\text{mass of water}}{\text{mass of dry coffee grounds}}. \tag{1}$$

The brew ratio is a hugely important parameter for brewing, and as we shall discover it turns out that small changes in R_{brew} can yield large changes in taste. For this initial brew, you want to use R_{brew} somewhere between 14 and 19. As an example, if you put in 20 grams of coffee grounds, you'll want to add 300 grams of cold water to get a brew ratio of 15. Remember: **the higher the brew ratio, the weaker the coffee!** (Refer to Appendix A and Appendix B for a concise summary of brewing and useful conversion factors.)

Watch the brewer carefully as it operates. Most importantly, think about the movement of the water as it moves up from the reservoir and then onto the grounds. Keep this question in mind: what causes the water to move up? Pour your brew into cups and turn off and unplug the Mr. Coffee. Taste the resulting coffee. What are your qualitative impressions? Refer to the "coffee flavor wheel" – can you detect any specific flavor notes? (Refer back to Lab 0 for a guide to tasting coffee.)

Data for the First Brew

Coffee type_____

Mass of water:_____ *grams*   Mass of beans:_____ *grams*

Brew Ratio (mass water per mass ground beans):

R_{brew} = _____ ÷ _____ = _____

Sensory Evaluations (how does the brew smell and taste?):

_____

_____

Hypothesis for why the water moves:

_____

_____

Part B – Partial Disassembly of a Drip Brewer

Once the Mr. Coffee is cool enough to handle, we will partially disassemble it to figure out how it works. Refer to the instructions and the guided questions below.

1) Turn off and unplug the brewer. Remove the spent grounds and put the glass carafe somewhere to the side. After the Mr. Coffee maker is cool enough to safely handle, turn the Mr. Coffee upside and use the provided screwdriver to remove the rubber feet and 6 screws on the bottom. Don't lose the feet or screws! Put them into an empty coffee cup.

2) Remove the bottom plate, and carefully inspect the interior of the Mr. Coffee. Try to identify each of the components visible underneath. Discuss with your group mates what mechanism you think there is for making the water move up to the grounds. Take a look at the various tubes that connect the cold water reservoir to the upper basket where the ground coffee is placed. **IMPORTANT: Do not attempt to remove anything or further disassemble the Mr. Coffee, this will likely break it.**

3) Take photos! While the Mr. Coffee is still opened up, have at least one person in your group take a photo of the interior of the Mr. Coffee. Also take one from the side and one from the top looking inside (with the lid open) at the reservoir and grounds basket. These photos are necessary for your lab report.

4) After you are satisfied with your photos, and after you think you understand what causes the water to move up, review the guided questions and identify the key components listed on pages 12-13.

5) Reassemble the Mr. Coffee.

Reverse Engineering Notes

After you remove the bottom of the drip brewer, carefully examine (and photograph) the interior. Recall all the important components are listed on page 20.

(i) First, trace the path of the water.

Are there any pumps or moving parts inside? _____

Look for a "check valve" inside of the rubber tubing. Which way does the check valve let the water flow?

_____

(ii) Next, let's examine the electrical circuitry.

Where is the electrical heater? _____

Why do you think it is located there, instead of where you pour the water in, or next to the check valve?

_____

You should see two electrical wires connected to opposite sides of the heater. Why are there two wires? Why can't just one wire deliver the electricity?

_____

Reverse Engineering Notes (continued)

There is at least one "fuse" between the heater and the wires leading to the electrical plug, and there likely is a "thermostat" attached to the heater. Why do you think the fuses and thermostat are there? What purposes do they serve?

_____

_____

(iii) After having looked at both the path of the water and the electrical components, what do you think forces the water to move up to the spray head? Do you think it boils and floats up as steam? How would you check this? If the water is not moving up as steam, what would make the hot water move up? (Think about what happens when bubbles expand... when you vaporize liquid water, it increases in volume by more than a factor of 500!) If the check valve wasn't there, what do you think would happen when you try to brew coffee?

_____

_____

_____

_____

Part C – Second Brew with Temperature Measurements

Finally, brew a second batch of coffee with two goals: measuring the masses of water, dry grounds, brew, and wet grounds carefully, and testing any hypotheses your group generated regarding the mechanism for how the water moved up against gravity. You will find a thermometer helpful! If the first brew was too "weak" or "strong" you may want to adjust your coffee to water ratio or the grind size to improve your second brew.

1) Carefully measure the mass of ground coffee you put into the Mr. Coffee, and carefully measure the mass of water you put in.

2) Measure the temperature in an appropriate location versus time during the entire brewing process. Hint: to understand why the water moves up to the spray nozzle, measure the temperature of the water dripping out of the spray nozzle. Recording every 15 seconds is recommended (see next page for template). What does the temperature tell you? (Recall the boiling point of water is 100°C.) After you're done brewing, measure the mass of coffee in the carafe. Also carefully weigh the moist "spent" grounds. Did the grounds gain or lose mass during the brewing? How much drinkable coffee did you get?

3) Does the second batch taste similar to the first? If not, why not? Again, refer to the coffee flavor wheel and the tasting guide in Lab 0.

Data and Tasting Notes for Second Brew

Coffee type:_____

Mass of empty carafe: _____ *grams*

Mass of water:_____ *grams*   Mass of beans:_____ *grams* R_{brew} :_____

Combined mass of plastic basket and filter paper: _____ *grams*

Mass of carafe with brewed coffee: _____ *grams*

Actual mass of brewed coffee = mass of carafe with brewed coffee – mass empty carafe

Actual mass of brewed coffee = _____ – _____ = _____ *grams*

Combined mass of plastic basket, filter paper and spent moist grounds: _____ *grams*

Actual mass of spent moist grounds: _____ – _____ = _____ *grams*

Sensory Evaluations: _____

_____

Temperature Data for Second Brew

Make sure the thermocouple is plugged in correctly into the meter. The big prong goes in the big hole. If the temperature goes down or negative, it's backwards!

Time (seconds)	Temperature (°C)	Time (seconds)	Temperature (°C)
_____ (first drips)	_____	_____	_____
_____	_____	_____	_____
_____	_____	_____	_____
_____	_____	_____	_____
_____	_____	_____	_____
_____	_____	_____	_____
_____	_____	_____	_____
_____	_____	_____	_____
_____	_____	_____	_____

(Last time recorded should correspond to the last drips delivered.)

Lab Report

By your specified due date, each group will submit their lab report that includes four main required parts: (1) labeled photos of the Mr. Coffee, (2) a qualitative process flow diagram, (3) a labeled scatter plot of temperature versus time, and (4) a brief paragraph discussing the mechanism for moving the water up in a Mr. Coffee.

(1) Open a new file in PowerPoint, and then import your best three photos of the Mr. Coffee: one from the side, one from the top looking under the lid, and one looking at the inside from underneath. Next, label all of the components and different parts of the Mr. Coffee. Use bright red arrows and easily readable text. (Hint: important labels include "heating element," "check valve" and "fuse.") Underneath each label, put a brief description (one phrase or one sentence max) of the purpose of that component or part. (Use a smaller but still legible font for the description.) You should end up with about a dozen unique labels.

(2) Sketch a "process flow diagram" for the brewing of coffee. Start with roasted coffee beans, and end with a final carafe full of coffee. An example process flow diagram (for doing laundry) is on page 21. Each unit operation can simply be a labeled rectangle (e.g., "grinder", "filter", etc.), but more importantly include labeled arrows showing **all** material streams entering and leaving each unit operation. Don't forget waste streams (e.g., the spent moist grounds). Most importantly, record your measurements of the masses of ground coffee and water you put into the Mr. Coffee, and the masses of what came out (moist spent grounds and drinkable coffee). You will be doing this more carefully in Lab 2. Import your sketch into your Powerpoint.

(3) Review Appendix C, which has tips on plotting and analyzing data. Then, use Excel to enter your measured temperature data, and generate a "scatter plot" of your temperature versus time. Make sure you label your axes, with proper units! For the title of the plot, indicate precisely where the temperature was measured. Copy your scatter plot into PowerPoint on a separate slide.

(4) On a final separate slide, insert a text box and write a brief paragraph (10 sentences max) that clearly answers the following questions: What causes the water to move upward? Why is there a check valve? What does your temperature data indicate regarding the mechanism? Why do you think the designers of the Mr. Coffee chose this approach for heating and moving the water?

Lab 1 Bonus Box – Caffeine the Wonder Drug

Coffee, tea, soda, chocolate - there are a lot of different ways to get your caffeine fix. But what is caffeine? In chemistry terms, it's an "organic" molecule composed of carbon, nitrogen, oxygen, and hydrogen, arranged in the molecular structure shown at right. Here we use the word "organic" in the chemistry sense that the compound contains carbon, not that it was a food grown without pesticides (as you find the word used in grocery stores). The formula might look intimidating, but caffeine is a natural substance: many different plants, including *Coffea arabica*, produce caffeine as a defense mechanism against insects. Happily, caffeine has positive psychoactive effects on mammals: reduced drowsiness, faster and clearer flow of thought, increased focus, better body coordination.

How much caffeine do you consume when you drink a cup of coffee? Well, each 8 ounce cup of coffee has between 75 to 175 milligrams (mg) of caffeine, depending mostly on how it was brewed and a little on how it was roasted. A rule of thumb is about 100 mg caffeine per cup of coffee. Caffeine is "generally regarded as safe," since the lethal dose is about 10 grams. You would have to chug about 100 cups in a row to hit that dosage!

In comparison to coffee, a typical cola (diet or regular) has a meager 25 to 45 mg of caffeine. Black tea has about 50 mg, while green tea has about 25 mg (all based on 8 ounce cups). Typical dark chocolate, say 70%, has about 80 mg per 2 ounces, or a whopping 320 mg if you ate a full 8 ounces (which is a half-pound of chocolate!) Caffeine in chocolate comes from the amount of cocoa "bean" (still a seed like coffee beans) in the chocolate; so the darker the chocolate, the higher the cocoa bean content and the greater the caffeine. The average adult consumes 300 mg of caffeine per day from all sources.

One reason for the range of caffeine levels in coffee is due to differences between the caffeine content in *arabica* vs. *robusta* coffee beans (another variety of *Coffea*). Specialty or gourmet coffees are typically *arabica* because it is considered to have a much better flavor profile. This is partially because *arabica* contains about half as much of caffeine and twice as much sucrose (sugar) compared to *robusta*. (The sucrose plays a key role in many of the roasting reactions that yield awesome flavors.) *Robusta* is definitely more "robust," with about 2.7% caffeine by mass to *arabica's* 1.5%. If you drink instant coffee it is likely *robusta*. In fact about 75% of the coffee cultivated worldwide is *arabica* because of the better taste and higher selling price.

Now why is caffeine considered a "Wonder Drug"? Believe it or not, some of the most extensive research on the effects of caffeine was carried out by various branches of the armed forces. In a military situation, staying alert could be a life or death proposition. Compared to other stimulants, caffeine is considered one of the safest – it has extremely low incidences of abuse and adverse health effects, it is a substance most people have experience with, it is known to help alleviate sleep deprivation-induced cognitive impairment, and it even improves strength and endurance. When you drink a caffeinated beverage or take a capsule, it takes about 30 to 45 minutes to have the full effects. To overcome this delay Wrigley and the Walter Reed Army Institute of Research developed "Stay Alert" caffeinated chewing gum which reaches your system in 5 to 10 minutes – a significant advantage if you need a quick pick-me-up.

Lab 2 – Process Flow Diagram & Mass Balances for Coffee

Objectives: The overarching goal of this lab is to answer the question, "Where does the initial mass of green coffee beans ultimately end up when you make coffee?" Toward this end, we will carefully measure the mass of each material stream through both the roasting and brewing processes, to make a complete process flow diagram that includes all unit operations.

Equipment:

☐ Mr. Coffee ☐ Nesco Roaster ☐ Colander and brush ☐ Graduated Cylinder

Activities:

☐ Part A – four brews in the Mr. Coffee, to determine mass balances and R_{abs}

☐ Part B – one roast in the Nesco, to measure mass and volume changes

Report:

☐ Quantitative process flow diagram, with mass balances

☐ Summary of mass balance calculations

☐ Scatter plot of m_{brew} vs. $m_{grounds}$, with best fit slope for R_{abs}

☐ Photos of your roast showing volume change

☐ Paragraph discussing key questions about the lab

Background

A "unit operation" is any step in a process where a chemical or physical change takes place. For example, a roaster induces a variety of chemical reactions to occur in the green beans; a grinder changes the average size of the roasted beans; a brewer extracts the hopefully tasty coffee molecules into the hot water. Each of these can be considered a "unit operation," but even within a single piece of equipment there can be multiple unit operations. A drip brewer combines the unit operations of heating, extraction, and filtration in one compact unit.

A fundamental aspect of every unit operation, regardless of how big or small, is that **mass must be conserved**. In other words, if we put 100 grams into a unit operation, ultimately we must get 100 grams out. This might sound very obvious. Things get tricky,

however, if we have multiple streams of mass moving into and out of the same unit operation. For example, a drip coffee brewer has two streams moving into it – ground coffee and cold water – but three streams moving out of it – (1) coffee to drink, (2) moist spent grounds, and (3) volatile gasses (steam, carbon dioxide, and volatile organic compounds or VOCs). The existence of these other two streams has a profound consequence: if we put in 300 grams of cold water into the brewer, we **don't** get 300 grams of coffee to drink! Some of the water is "lost" to the other waste streams.

So, if we want to design a process to make a large quantity of coffee (say 1 liter of coffee for the design competition), we must first analyze how mass flows through the system. The crucial question is: how much water and coffee grounds should we put in to get a certain amount of brewed coffee? Likewise, how much coffee should we roast?

Mass Balance for Water in Brewing

Let's focus first on the mass of water in the drip brewer. In words, our equation for conservation of mass is

$$Mass\ of\ Water\ In = Mass\ of\ Water\ Out. \tag{1}$$

Recognizing that we have one stream of water feed in, but three streams that contain water feed out, equation (1) means we have

$$m_{feed} = m_{brew} + m_{spent} + m_{evap}. \tag{2}$$

Here m_{feed} is the mass of cold water put into the brewer, m_{brew} is the mass of water in the brewed coffee, m_{spent} is the mass of <u>water</u> in the moist spent grounds, and m_{evap} is the mass of water lost as evaporated steam (water vapor) into the atmosphere. Importantly, in this balance each of these terms refers only to the mass of water in that stream, so m_{spent} is not the combined mass of solid coffee and water in the moist spent grounds – it's only the water mass.

Equation (2) isn't so useful yet, but it turns out we can make some very helpful simplifying assumptions. First, under most circumstances the mass lost to evaporation is pretty small, so we can neglect it. (You will test whether this is a good assumption in this lab.) Second, it turns out that brewed coffee is about 99% water, i.e., the coffee solids dissolved in the brew are only about 1% by mass. So for now, we will ignore the mass of coffee solids in the brew and just approximate it as all water mass. (As we shall see in Lab 5, another mass balance applies to the coffee solids, and we can determine the mass of coffee solids extracted into the brewed coffee.)

Third, and most importantly, we need to know how much water gets "left behind" in the spent grounds. The initially dry coffee grounds have a finite capacity to "absorb" water, in much the same way a paper towel can only absorb so much water. To good approximation the mass of water absorbed into the spent grounds is simply proportional to the initial mass of dry coffee grounds, i.e.,

$$m_{spent} = R_{abs} \times m_{grounds}. \tag{3}$$

Here R_{abs} is the "absorption ratio" that describes the ratio of how many grams of water are absorbed in the moistened grounds, per gram of initial dry coffee grounds, i.e.,

$$R_{abs} = \frac{\text{mass of water absorbed into the coffee grounds}}{\text{initial mass of dry coffee grounds}} \tag{4}$$

If we substitute Eq. (3) into Eq. (2), and neglect the mass lost to evaporation, we obtain the very useful prediction

$$m_{brew} = m_{feed} - (R_{abs} \times m_{grounds}). \qquad (5)$$

In other words, if we want to know **how much drinkable coffee we're going to get**, we need to know three things:

i) how much cold water
ii) how much dry coffee grounds
iii) the numerical value of R_{abs}

A key goal of this lab is for you to measure R_{abs} experimentally, by systematically varying the mass of dry grounds but with a fixed amount of cold water. Instead of calculating R_{abs} for each individual brew, we will perform a more accurate procedure. Equation (5) is what's known as a "linear equation," of the form you likely studied in high school. A plot of how much drinkable coffee you get (m_{brew}) on the vertical axis versus how much dry grounds you used ($m_{grounds}$) on the horizontal axis will yield a straight line. The intercept of this plot will be m_{feed}, and the slope will be equal to $-R_{abs}$. (You can refer to Appendix C for tips and advice on plotting.) This procedure effectively yields what's known as a "best fit" value for R_{abs}.

Mass Balance for Roasting

To complete our process flow diagram, we also need to think about roasting. The principle of conservation of mass equally applies to roasting:

$$\textit{Mass of Coffee In} = \textit{Mass of Coffee Out}. \qquad (6)$$

Just like for brewing, in roasting there are multiple streams that exit the roaster. Obviously you have the roasted beans. As you will see during your first roast, you also have the "chaff," which is the fragile skins of the green coffee beans that flake off during the early stages of the roast. The chaff is usually collected by a filter screen of some sort in the exhaust from the roaster (much like the lint screen in a clothes dryer).

Finally, the least obvious stream of mass exiting the roaster is the escaping gasses. In our brewing mass balance we neglected the volatile gasses because they were so small. Roasting, in contrast, reaches much higher temperatures, and it turns out that a very significant fraction of mass is lost as water vapor, carbon dioxide, and other VOCs formed during the roasting reactions.

Putting everything together, equation (6) becomes

$$m_{green} = m_{roasted} + m_{chaff} + m_{gas}, \qquad (7)$$

where m_{green} is the initial mass of green beans, $m_{roasted}$ is the mass of roasted beans afterwards, m_{chaff} is the mass of chaff collected during roasting, and m_{gas} is the collective mass of all the gasses that escaped during roasting.

The first three masses are easy to measure, but m_{gas} cannot be directly measured. That's ok – you will measure it indirectly in this lab!

Part A – Mass Balances for Brewing

1) First, weigh out about 70 grams of roasted coffee beans and then grind all of them together at the same time. This ensures a uniform grind size for all experiments in Part A.

2) Weigh the empty glass carafe and an empty plastic basket (with a dry filter paper inside of it). You will need these weights later.

3) Pour 300 grams of cold water into the Mr. Coffee, and place 20 grams of your ground coffee in the filter basket. (Set the other 45 grams to the side.) Before you begin brewing, however, weigh the entire Mr. Coffee and record the mass. **Make sure the electrical cord is unplugged and draped over the top of the Mr. Coffee**; otherwise your mass measurements will vary with how much tension is on the cord. You will eventually compare this initial mass to the mass after the brewing is done. What will these numbers tell you about the mass of lost gases (like steam)?

4) After the Mr. Coffee is done brewing, weigh the entire mass of the Mr. Coffee, and then separately weigh the glass carafe (with coffee) as well as the combined mass of the plastic basket (with moist spent grounds).

5) Go ahead and taste the coffee – how does it taste?

Repeat steps (3) and (5) for three more brews. Each time, use exactly 300 grams of cold water, but vary the mass of ground coffee beans. Recommended: second brew, use 30 grams; third brew, use 10 grams, fourth and final brew, use 5 grams. Make sure you carefully record the mass of brewed coffee each time. How does the brew ratio affect the taste?

Data for First Brew (and Flow Diagram)

Coffee type_____

Mass of empty glass carafe: _____ *grams*

Combined mass of plastic basket and filter paper: _____ *grams*

Mass of cold water:_____ *grams* Mass of beans:_____ *grams* $R_{brew}=$_____

Mass of entire Mr. Coffee (with water and grounds) **before** brewing: _____ *grams*

Mass of entire Mr. Coffee (with water and grounds) **after** brewing: _____ *grams*

Mass lost to evaporation: _____ – _____ = _____ *grams*

Mass of carafe with brewed coffee: _____ *grams*

Actual mass of brewed coffee: _____ – _____ = _____ *grams*

Combined mass of plastic basket, moist filter and spent moist grounds: _____ *grams*

Actual mass of spent moist grounds: _____ – _____ = _____ *grams*

Sensory Evaluations: _____

_____

Lab 2

Data for Second Brew

Mass of cold water:_____ *grams*   Mass of beans:_____ *grams* R_{brew}=_____

Mass of carafe with brewed coffee: _____ *grams*

Actual mass of brewed coffee: _____ − _____ = _____ *grams*

Sensory Evaluations:

_____

_____

Data for Third Brew

Mass of cold water:_____ *grams*   Mass of beans:_____ *grams* R_{brew}=_____

Mass of carafe with brewed coffee: _____ *grams*

Actual mass of brewed coffee: _____ − _____ = _____ *grams*

Sensory Evaluations:

_____

_____

Data for Fourth Brew

Mass of cold water:_____ *grams*   Mass of beans:_____ *grams* R_{brew}=_____

Mass of carafe with brewed coffee: _____ *grams*

Actual mass of brewed coffee: _____ − _____ = _____ *grams*

Sensory Evaluations:

_____

_____

 **Safety note:** Don't put too many green beans into the Nesco roaster – and don't put too few! Note the two fill lines... if you put in too many beans they will not circulate properly and they will catch on fire. Likewise, if you put in too few, they will get too hot too quickly and likely catch on fire. The safe range is **100 to 130 grams** of green coffee beans. Do not leave your roaster unattended for any reason. If you see lots of smoke, stop the roast!

Part B – Mass Balances for Roasting

1) After you feel adequately caffeinated, it's time to turn to roasting. Review the safety guidelines for proper use of the Nesco roaster. Carefully weigh out 125 grams of green coffee beans, and place them in the graduated cylinder – what volume do they occupy? Take a picture of your green beans in the graduated cylinder, using a white piece of paper for background. Don't worry about washing the cylinder after you're done.

2) Do a light roast, about 18-20 minutes. The last five minutes of the roast (in the Nesco) is a cooling cycle, so the real roast time is 13 to 15 minutes. **Observe the beans as they roast!** Proper roast time is highly dependent on the beans' moisture and the specific electrical line voltage, which can vary considerably from one outlet to another. Try to listen for the first crack and **observe the color** – this will tell you more than the timer!

3) After the roast cooling cycle is complete, carefully dump the roasted beans into the metal mesh colander. Important: for this lab you need to weigh all chaff! (In subsequent labs we won't need to worry about it.) Carefully collect the chaff that falls through the mesh, and also carefully brush out the chaff from the filter basket inside the roaster. Weigh the collected chaff, and weigh the roasted coffee beans. Is the chaff weight appreciable or negligible? (Note many scales have a minimum weight tolerance – the chaff by itself won't register unless you use a heavy enough container.)

4) Pour the roasted beans back into the graduated cylinder. What volume do they now occupy? How much have they expanded? Take a picture of the roasted beans in the

Roasting Data

Coffee type_____

Mass of green beans:_____ *grams*   Volume of green beans:_____ mL

Time spent roasting (including cooling cycle): _____ *minutes*

Mass of roasted beans:_____ *grams*   Volume of roasted beans:_____ mL

Mass of chaff:_____ *grams*

Mass lost as volatile gasses: _____ – _____ – _____ = _____ *grams*

Note and observations: _____

_____

graduated cylinder. What type of roast would you characterize your beans as? Feel free to taste one (they're edible.)

5) Once the roasted beans are <u>completely cool</u>, place them into a storage bag, and write your group's name, section number, and sample number on it. Warm beans can partially melt the bag causing unpleasant flavors – be patient!

Lab Report

By your specified due date, each group will submit their lab report that includes (1) a quantitative process flow diagram that reflects the mass balances on the different material streams, (2) summary of mass balance calculations, (3) a scatter plot of m_{brew} vs. $m_{grounds}$, (4) labeled "before/after" photos of your roast, and (5) a brief paragraph discussing your group's observations.

(1) Open your qualitative "coffee process flow diagram" from last week, and make any modifications as necessary to it so that it is a complete diagram, including roasting (cf. the discussion on page 13). Using the data from your first brew, your group will then start inserting your quantitative mass measurements (numerical values). We will focus here only on the coffee solids and water streams – do not worry about air, CO_2, or VOCs. Make sure you include appropriate units (e.g., grams) with each number you insert! Start with green coffee beans, and end with a final cup of coffee. You will find that you roasted more beans than you could use in one brew, which is OK. Just indicate that the difference goes to "storage," so that your masses balance out.

(2) The second page should be your calculations to obtain the mass measurements. What you measured in lab should be clearly identified, and your calculations should be easy to follow. It is OK if you hand write this page and then scan or photograph it to insert into PowerPoint, but you will probably find it easier to use Excel (cf. step 3).

(3) In Excel, use your experimental data to generate a scatter plot of m_{brew} (on the vertical axis) versus $m_{grounds}$ (on the horizontal axis). Use the built-in line fitting to make a "best-fit" line and determine the slope. As discussed on page 30 the slope of this line is the negative of R_{abs}. (Refer to Appendix C for important Excel tips.)

(4) On the next page of your report, insert your "before/after" photos of the roasted beans. Make sure they're clearly labeled! What is the <u>percent</u> volume change?

(5) On a final separate slide, insert a text box and write a paragraph that clearly answers the following questions:

(i) What did your experiments tell you about the absorption ratio during brewing? What numerical value did you get for R_{abs}? As a specific example, if you start with 600 grams of cold water, how much drinkable coffee would you get if you used 50 grams of ground coffee?

(ii) How much water was lost to steam during the brewing? Is this water lost to steam a significant or negligible fraction of the overall water mass balance?

(iii) How much mass of initial green coffee beans do you "lose" during roasting? What fraction is the chaff? Where does the rest of the mass go? Do you think this answer will be the same for light and dark roasts?

Lab 2 Bonus Box – What happens to spent coffee grounds?

Every time you brew coffee, you are left with two things – hopefully the first is a great cup of coffee; the second is spent coffee grounds. We all know what to do with a great cup of coffee, but what can be done with spent coffee grounds? You definitely don't want to rebrew them, because you have already removed about 2/3 of the soluble coffee from the grounds (that's the 18 to 22% percent extraction that you will learn about in Lab 5). What's left behind are less desirable flavor molecules that take longer to extract and will not enhance your next brew.

If you go on-line, there are a wealth of resources and ideas for uses of spent coffee grounds. First, spent coffee grounds are a great fertilizer, especially if your soil is alkaline (pH>7). Most plants prefer soil pH to be between 6 to 7. Acid loving plants include cucumbers, eggplant, carrots, roses, and hydrangeas (which happen to be pH sensitive and turn a lovely purplish blue when fertilized with coffee). The grounds are also thought to keep some insects (ants, slugs, and snails) and even the neighbor's cat from using your garden as a litter box. Spent coffee grounds also can be used in your kitchen refrigerator or freezer as a deodorizer and are a handy way to keep worms alive for fishing or aid their digestion in the compost heap. But the uses don't stop there: spent grounds can even be part of your beauty regimen as an exfoliate (body scrub), face mask, or added to some shampoo to help remove styling product residue from hair.

These sorts of uses are great at the home scale where you might generate 100 grams of spent coffee grounds each day. Your local coffee house generates 10 to 50 pounds per day, though, and manufacturers can generate thousands of pounds of spent coffee grounds every day. For example, one medium size Bay Area cold brew coffee company we like produces 15,000 to 20,000 pounds of spent coffee grounds – per day! To put this on an even grander scale, Americans consume about 400 million cups of coffee per day, which corresponds to a staggering 24 million pounds of spent coffee grounds, each and every single day of the year.

Unfortunately, most of the spent grounds end up in landfills. Just as you might find it difficult to get every possible use out of your spent coffee grounds, coffee houses and companies have a difficult time, as well. That Bay Area manufacturer offers their spent coffee grounds for free to anyone who can find a way to use them. Unfortunately, few take them up on their offer.

This is a shame, because the spent coffee grounds contain useful chemicals not completely removed during brewing – such as remaining aromatic flavor compounds, lipids and fats, proteins, minerals, and phenolic antioxidants, which could be removed and used in other products. The bulk of the material, however, is cellulosic (plant cell walls). Cellulose and hemicellulose can be used as feedstocks for biorefineriers, but with crude oil (petroleum) so inexpensive, biorefining of coffee grounds isn't profitable. Simply burning the spent grounds for energy is difficult as the grounds must be dry and burning them generates a lot of particulates, which are not good for air quality. The engineering challenge is to develop an environmentally sound and economically viable process. As more research is done, new treatments, processes, and uses may become available to improve the situation. Indeed, a completely integrated use/exploitation processing system where every valuable component is extracted and used optimally is possible with existing technology – and with further engineering work, should someday be economically viable.

Lab 3 – The pH of Coffee and Chemical Reactions

Objectives: In this lab, we will consider how the pH (the acidity) of brewed coffee depends on the roast level, and how the pH changes with time after brewing to estimate a "reaction rate." We will also do some more roasts to prepare for the next lab.

Equipment:

☐ Clever Coffee ☐ Electric kettle ☐ Mr. Coffee ☐ pH meter ☐ paper cups

☐ Nesco roaster

Activities:

☐ Part A – two Mr. Coffee brews

  ☐ First brew and systematic sampling of pH over 75 minutes

  ☐ Second brew at 75 minutes to do blind taste test comparison

☐ Part B – two Clever Coffee brews, to compare the pH of a commercial dark roast and your light roast from Lab 2

☐ Part C – two roasts in the Nesco (one dark, one light) for the next lab

Report:

☐ Scatter plot of pH vs. time

☐ Estimate of the *rate* of the chemical reaction

☐ Tasting notes and pH of light roast vs. dark roast

☐ Paragraph discussing key questions about the lab

Background

Imagine that you carefully roast some high quality green beans, and a couple days later you carefully brew them. You taste it, and you think it's absolutely the best coffee you've ever made. Excited, you text your friend and invite them over. Half an hour later your friend arrives, but the response when they taste your coffee is a polite "I guess it's OK." Confused, you taste it again, and you agree… now it tastes mediocre. What happened?

A key thing to realize about coffee is that the taste of any given brew will change with time. The moment the hot water hits the coffee grounds, three processes start occurring. The first process is "mass transfer," which is the migration of the molecules out of the solid phase (ground beans) and into the liquid phase (water). This change is manifested as an obvious change in the color of the water, from transparent to dark. (We examine mass transfer in more detail in Lab 5.) This process stops once you separate the grounds from the brew.

Two other processes, however, continue to occur. The second process is the escape of volatile organic compounds (VOCs) from the liquid phase into the gas phase. These VOCs comprise the wonderful aromas that you smell while brewing coffee; over 1000 unique different molecules have been identified as contributing to the aroma of coffee. As long as the coffee is exposed to the open atmosphere, the VOCs will continue to volatilize and escape. The VOCs in the brew are eventually depleted, so the wonderful coffee aroma disappears, and the taste suffers.

The third process involves chemical reactions. This process is much less obvious, and most people have no idea it occurs. Even though it might look like your coffee pot is just sitting there with motionless coffee, in reality a bewildering variety of complicated reactions are taking place within the coffee. Some of these reactions generate new VOCs; others consume them. In particular, several chemical reactions release additional acidic molecules. Some acidity is good: coffee aficionados highly value coffees that yield a pleasant acidity, or "brightness," in their coffee. (Here the term "brightness" has nothing to do with how it looks visually!) Too much acidity, however, makes the coffee taste increasingly sour. This is the primary reason that coffee sitting on a hot plate for a long time tastes "stale" or "sour."

Although the chemical reactions are complex, they have an easily measured effect on the brew: the pH of the brew changes with time. Recall that pH is a measure of the acid concentration in a solution, defined as

$$\text{pH} = -\log_{10}[H_3O^+], \tag{1}$$

where $[H_3O^+]$ is the concentration, in moles/liter, of "hydronium ions." A hydronium ion is basically a water molecule with an extra hydrogen atom attached to it, giving it a net positive charge. Note that the pH is a logarithmic scale. Distilled water has a pH of 7, which means the hydronium concentration is 10^{-7} mol/L. In contrast, the vinegar you buy at the store has a pH closer to 4, so the hydronium ion concentration is 10^{-4} mol/L. The difference between pH 4 and pH 7 might seem small numerically, but it's a logarithmic scale: the vinegar is $10^3 = 1000$ times more acidic.

As an example calculation, let's say you measure a coffee with pH = 5.2. The actual hydronium concentration is

$$[H_3O^+] = 10^{-5.2}\,\tfrac{\text{mol}}{\text{L}} = 0.0000063\,\tfrac{\text{mol}}{\text{L}} = 6.3 \times 10^{-6}\,\tfrac{\text{mol}}{\text{L}}. \tag{2}$$

Don't be fooled by the seemingly small number: the human tongue can definitely detect the acid associated with such small concentrations!

What sets the pH of coffee? The initial pH upon brewing will depend on several factors, including the variety of beans, how they were roasted (light vs. dark), as well as the initial pH of the water you use to brew. If the initial pH of the water is slightly basic (say around 8), then the initial pH of the brewed coffee might be around 6. With time, however, the chemical reactions keep generating more hydronium ions, and the pH will decrease, causing the coffee to taste increasingly sour. If it reaches a pH of 5, your coffee is now 10 times more acidic than when first brewed – with a very noticeable effect on taste! A main goal of Lab 3 is for you to measure the pH of a brew vs. time, and to compare your numerical pH measurements with corresponding sensory evaluations.

The pH changes because of a chemical reaction, so a natural question is, "How fast does the chemical reaction happen?" When we ask that question, what we really mean is "How many molecules per liter are produced per minute?" The coffee pot is effectively what chemical engineers refer to as a "batch reactor," so you can use the pH data to get an estimate for the rate of reaction as

$$\text{rate} = \frac{d}{dt}[H_3O^+] \approx \frac{\Delta [H_3O^+]}{\Delta \text{time}} \approx \frac{\text{change in } [H_3O^+]}{\text{change in time}} \approx \frac{[H_3O^+]_{final} - [H_3O^+]_{init}}{t_{elapsed}}, \quad (3)$$

where "init" means the initial hydronium concentration (at $t = 0$), "final" means your final concentration, and $t_{elapsed}$ is the amount of time (in minutes) until your final measurement. Note that the rate has units of moles per liter per minute, i.e., mol/(L×min). Also note that the above expression is only a rough estimate (because we approximate the time derivative), but that's OK if we only need an estimate… we call it an "engineering approximation."

Part A – Measuring the pH versus time

Important: you need to multitask during this experiment – get part A started, and then simultaneously start working on part B then part C.

1) Get ready to make some coffee in the Mr. Coffee, using **dark** roasted coffee. Prepare a large amount: use about 600 grams of water, and 40 grams of coffee ($R_{brew} = 15$). Measure the pH of the water that you put into the brewer. As soon as you start the Mr. Coffee, note the time (you will eventually be plotting pH versus time, so keep track of what time you pull samples). Keep a record of how you prepare the brew – you will do it again at the end for a comparison taste test of "fresh" vs "stale" coffee.

2) As soon as it's done brewing, pour out **small** samples to taste (about 1 ounce max), and try to assess the "brightness" or perceived acidity of the coffee. How does it taste? Write the time you poured the sample on the side of the paper cup.

3) Next, review the warnings below about proper usage of handheld pH meters. They typically only provide an accurate pH when the coffee is cool – don't try to measure the pH of steaming hot coffee! To do this, pour a little bit of coffee in a small paper cup or glass mug, let it cool down for a few minutes, then measure the temperature to confirm it is less than 40 °C. Only then insert the pH probe, wait 10 seconds, then record the pH. Record the pH of the brew sample.

4) For the next 75 minutes, **keep the glass carafe on the hot plate** with the Mr. Coffee on, and take a small sample and pH measurement every 5 minutes. (A cell phone timer might be useful here.) You can taste every time if you like, but the changes will be gradual – instead focus on taking small tastes at the 30 minute and 60 minute marks. How has the perceived acidity changed with time compared to the initial brew?

5) At the end of the 75 minutes, set aside the remaining stale coffee for a blind taste test. Prepare another batch of coffee to brew, using exactly the same procedure as your first brew. As soon as your second batch of coffee is brewed, do a blind tasting of the 'stale' coffee versus the 'fresh' coffee. Can you taste a difference? Measure the pH.

Special warnings about handheld pH meters:
1) DO NOT push the "CAL" button (this changes the calibration!)
2) DO NOT submerge the buttons in coffee or water – only the tip!
3) Always measure room temperature coffee, between 20 to 40°C.
4) Rinse and gently dry the pH probe tip between readings.

pH versus Time Data

Coffee type_____

Mass of water:_____ *grams*   Mass of beans:_____ *grams* R_{brew}:_____

pH of tap water: _____

pH of coffee at end of brew: _____   (This is your pH at time=0.)

Time (minutes)	pH	Time (minutes)	pH
_____	_____	_____	_____
_____	_____	_____	_____
_____	_____	_____	_____
_____	_____	_____	_____
_____	_____	_____	_____
_____	_____	_____	_____
_____	_____	_____	_____
_____	_____	_____	_____

Sensory Evaluations at **t=0 (end of brew)**:   pH = _____

_____

_____

Sensory Evaluations at **t=30 minutes**:   pH = _____

_____

_____

Sensory Evaluations at **t=60 minutes**:   pH = _____

_____

_____

Sensory Evaluations at **t=75 minutes**:   pH = _____

_____

_____

Sensory Data for Second Brew & Blind Taste Notes

Sensory Evaluations at t=0 (end of brew):   pH = _____

_____

_____

Blind tasting comparison notes:

_____

_____

_____

Part B – Measuring the pH of your light roast vs. a dark roast

1) Our next task will be to do a head-to-head comparison of your light roast from Lab 2 vs. some store-bought dark roast. We will use a new brewing technique – set up two Clever Coffee Drippers. Do your best to grind the light roast and the dark roast to the same grind size, and add equal masses to either brewer. Use the electric kettle to heat water to 94°C, and brew each for the same amount of time (about 4 minutes).

2) Do a "blind" taste of the two brews. Let somebody else pour them for you so that you don't know which is which. How do they taste?

pH Data for Light vs. Dark Roast

LIGHT ROAST Type: _____

Mass of hot water: _____ *grams* Mass of grounds: _____ *grams* R_{brew}: _____

Grind: _____   Extraction time: _____ *minutes* Temperature water: _____ °C

pH of brew: _____   Sensory Evaluations:

_____

_____

DARK ROAST Type: _____

Mass of hot water: _____ *grams* Mass of grounds: _____ *grams* R_{brew}: _____

Grind: _____   Extraction time: _____ *minutes* Temperature water: _____ °C

pH of brew: _____   Sensory Evaluations:

_____

_____

Part C – Roasting a light and a dark roast

During the 75 minutes of your pH data acquisition, we will multi-task to also perform two roasts – a light roast and a dark roast, both with the same type of green beans. Use the exact same procedure as last week, but don't bother measuring the chaff or the volume change (those activities were only for Lab 2). **Observe the beans as they roast!** The timer doesn't tell you whether you'll get a dark or light roast, you have to watch them to see how they're doing. Make sure you let the roaster cool for about five minutes between roasts. Label and store your beans for next week. Remember, only bag fully cooled beans.

If you like, you can taste the roasted beans – can you taste a difference between the light and dark roast?

Roasting Data

Coffee type: _____

First Roast (Light)

Mass of green beans: _____ *grams*   Mass of roasted beans: _____ *grams*

Time spent roasting: _____ *minutes*

Sensory notes of the beans:

_____

_____

Second Roast (Dark)

Mass of green beans: _____ *grams*   Mass of roasted beans: _____ *grams*

Time spent roasting: _____ *minutes*

Sensory notes of the beans:

_____

_____

Lab Report

By your specified due date, each group will submit their lab report that includes (1) a plot of pH versus time, (2) an estimate of the reaction rate, (3) tasting notes and pH of light vs. dark roast, and (4) a brief paragraph discussing your group's observations.

(1) First, use Excel to generate a scatter plot of the pH versus time that you generated with the Mr. Coffee. (Put the pH on the vertical axis, and time on the horizontal axis.) What trends do you observe?

(2) Using equation (3), what is an estimate for the rate of reaction generating hydronium ions? If you let the coffee sit on the hot plate for three times as long (say 3 hours instead of 60 minutes), and if we assume the rate stayed constant (a huge assumption!), what would the final pH be?

(3) Next, write down your tasting notes for your Clever Coffee brews of the light and dark roasts, and their pH values. Qualitative taste impressions are fine! You can type if you like, or just scan your handwritten notes. Which did each group member prefer?

(4) On a final separate page, write a brief paragraph (10 sentences max) that clearly answers the following questions:

  (i) In absolute terms, how much more acidic was your light roast vs. your dark roast? In other words, how many more times hydronium ions were there? (Recall that a liquid with pH of 5 has ten times more hydronium ions than a liquid with pH 6.)

  (ii) How did the taste of the coffee vary with time as it sat on the heating plate? Qualitative impressions are fine! Did you notice a correlation with pH?

  (iii) How much did the concentration (in mol/L) of hydronium ions change while the coffee was sitting around for 75 minutes?

  (iv) What were the differences in taste between fresh coffee, and coffee that has sat around for 30, 60 and 75 minutes? Describe the blind taste outcome – how easy or difficult was it to identify the stale coffee versus the fresh coffee?

Lab 3 Bonus Box – What Happens During a Roast?

Roasting is a critical step towards obtaining "nirvana in a cup" quality coffee. There are a myriad of physical and chemical changes that occur when you roast green coffee beans, all triggered by heating the beans. Initially, green beans contain 10 to 13% water moisture. As the bean and water heat up, the water vaporizes. At a certain point near 200°C, the vapor pressure in the bean, due to the expansion of gases with temperature, is so large that the beans actually crack open. An audible crack or popping noise can be heard in some roasters. The cracking and fissures in the beans allow the water vapor and other gases to escape and also cause a significant increase in the volume of the bean. In the image above it is possible to see some of these cracks.

The same type of cracking happens when you pop popcorn. The corn kernels contain water and gases that heat up, and once the pressure exceeds the strength of the corn kernel shell – they explode. The cell walls of coffee beans are just tougher and less continuous, so that explosive event is less dramatic. Moreover, have you ever noticed that old corn kernels don't pop up that much? The reason is simply that the kernels have dried out and there isn't enough water in the kernel to build sufficient pressure to pop the kernel. If you add some water to the old bag and let it sit overnight, those kernels will absorb the moisture and pop much better the next day. As you keep heating coffee beans they even crack a second time starting around 225°C. This further opens up the bean and plant cell walls. As a result, oils in the bean migrate to the surface and cause the bean to appear shiny or oily.

But pops and cracks aren't all that is happening. Just like baking or roasting other foods, there are a host of complex chemical reactions that also occur as the beans heat up. The most obvious changes are from "Maillard" reactions, which result in the brown color of the roasted bean. Maillard reactions occur between proteins and sugars – just like when you toast bread. The other main type of chemical reaction is "pyrolysis," which is a general term that means a reaction caused by heat in the absence of oxygen – which occurs inside the bean. Pyrolysis caramelizes sugars and carbohydrates, and changes the fats in the bean to aromatic oils. If you have cooked food, you have carried out both Maillard and pyrolysis reactions, but hopefully not too much combustion! Yes, if you go too far with your coffee roast, you can actually burn the coffee beans, just like wood in a fireplace. Combustion reactions are caused by heat as well, but in the presence of oxygen. Combustion is not good in coffee!

Another important aspect of green coffee beans is that they contain a lot of chlorogenic acids, which make up 4-9% of the green beans. Why focus on this one type of molecule? Well, chlorogenic acids are found in a lot of plants, but what is special about them is that they are antioxidants. Roasting actually breaks down chlorogenic acids; in fact, only about 40% of these molecules remain in a medium roast and really dark roasts are down below 10%. So, lighter roasts are "brighter" (more acidic) and may actually be healthier.

If all these changes that occur during roasting are confusing for you to follow, you are not alone. There are so many different possible reactions during roasting that scientists still don't have a full handle on all that is going on either. Moreover, the composition of the green beans varies like any natural crop, so a roast that gives you "nirvana in a cup" using one type of green bean may lead to brown swill with another. But all is not lost: try different roasting levels and explore what yields the best tasting brew.

Lab 4 – Measuring the Energy Used to Make Coffee

Objectives: The overarching goal of this lab is to answer the question, "How much energy does it take to make coffee?" We will measure the heat capacity of water, and compare the energy requirements for brewing, roasting, and grinding.

Equipment:

☐ Electric kettle ☐ Kill-a-Watt meter ☐ Hot-air popcorn roaster ☐ Nesco roaster

☐ Clever Coffee Dripper

Activities:

☐ Part A – heating water in the electric kettle (twice), to determine C_p for water

☐ Part B – two brews (light and dark roast) using Clever Coffee Drippers

☐ Part C – measuring the energy of roasting

    ☐ First roast in hot-air popcorn roaster with qualitative observations

    ☐ Second roast with simultaneous temperature and energy measurements

    ☐ Third roast in Nesco for comparison

☐ Part D – measuring the energy of grinding

Report:

☐ Three scatter plots for heating water, of water temperature, energy, and time

☐ Table of calculations for C_p of water

☐ Two scatter plots for roasting, temperature vs. time and energy vs. time

☐ Column plot of energy per gram used by different unit operations

☐ Paragraphs discussing tasting notes and key questions about the lab

Background

Everybody has a qualitative idea of what "energy" means. When you are tired and sluggish after exercise, you say "I'm out of energy…" In contrast, when you move around quickly from task to task, you say "I have a lot of energy!" The idea of energy is clearly tied to motion, and indeed the most general definition of energy is "the ability to do work."

Energy exists in many different forms, all of which have a connection to motion or the ability to yield motion. For example, one kind of energy is "kinetic energy," which is the name we give to the energy of an object (say a baseball) moving through the air. Other kinds of energy have a much more subtle connection to motion. For example, "heat" is also a kind of energy, but

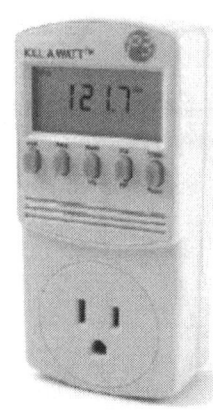

the motion isn't something you can observe like a baseball: instead the motion is the vibration of the molecules in whatever substance is holding the heat. A glass of cold water contains relatively little "heat" since the water molecules jiggle around sluggishly. In contrast, a glass of hot water contains more "heat" since the water molecules jiggle around vigorously.

A fundamental aspect of the universe is that energy is never created or destroyed. Instead, energy simply changes from one form to another. This idea, often referred to as "conservation of energy," means that we can precisely quantify how much energy is needed to accomplish certain goals, by transferring energy from one form to another. An example that is hugely important to modern society involves hydroelectric dams, where the kinetic energy of falling water is transferred to the kinetic energy of a spinning turbine; magnets inside the spinning turbine transfer the kinetic energy to electrical energy (i.e., electrons moving along a conducting wire). When you flip on a light switch in your home, the electrical energy is transferred yet again to light energy (which involves moving photons).

In each of these transferences of energy, the efficiency isn't 100%; typically some fraction of the energy is "lost" as heat energy to the surroundings. Think of that incandescent light bulb, which puts out light but also gets quite hot. Nonetheless, conservation of energy is absolute. Much like our mass balances from Lab 2, the total energy put in to any system must ultimately be equal to the energy pulled out of the system.

The standard unit of energy is named the "joule," after James Prescott Joule, a 19th century physicist (and professional beer brewer) who helped elucidate the idea of conservation of energy. To see what a joule of energy is, first we need to define the force necessary to put things into motion. Specifically, imagine you have a mass of 1 kilogram sitting around somewhere, and you want to accelerate it to 1 meter per second. You could either slowly accelerate it (by nudging it gently) or you could quickly accelerate it (by pushing hard). If you push it precisely hard enough so that it reaches 1 meter per second within exactly one second, then you have applied 1 "newton" of force,

$$1 \text{ newton} = 1 \text{ N} = 1 \ \frac{\text{kg} \times \text{m}}{\text{s}^2}. \tag{1}$$

The newton is of course named after Sir Isaac Newton, who developed the famous Newton's Laws of Motion. One joule of energy, then, is defined as the energy transferred when applying a force of 1 newton over a distance of 1 meter, i.e.,

$$1 \text{ joule} = 1 \text{ J} = 1 \text{ N} \times \text{m} = 1 \ \frac{\text{kg} \times \text{m}^2}{\text{s}^2}. \tag{2}$$

The *rate* at which you transfer energy is referred to as the "power," typically measured in watts, and is defined as how many joules you use per second,

$$1 \text{ watt} = 1 \text{ W} = 1 \text{ joule} / \text{second} = 1 \text{ J} / \text{s}. \tag{3}$$

The Watt is named after yet another famous engineer, Mr. James Watt, who helped develop the steam engines that powered the industrial revolution. In fact, Mr. Watt invented the idea of "horsepower," a still commonly used measure of power, since Watt's steam engines were replacing horses. We emphasize that the watt and horsepower are both a metric for describing a *rate* of energy per time, analogous to a metric for volumetric flow rate like gallons per second, or mass flow rate like kilograms per second.

What does all of this have to do with coffee? Well, energy is definitely required to convert green coffee beans into a drinkable beverage. For our purposes the most important type of energy transfer is of electrical energy to heat energy (since we need to heat the beans during roasting as well as heat the water for brewing). Electrical energy, like any other energy, is also measured in joules, and the power (or energy per time) is measured in watts.

If you go to a hardware store you might see that an incandescent light bulb for sale requires about 100 watts, which means it consumes 100 joules / second of electrical energy to operate. Let's say you buy the lightbulb, plug it in and leave the light on for one hour. Since there are 3600 seconds in one hour, this means that over the course of the hour the light bulb has used

$$100 \frac{\text{joule}}{\text{second}} \times 3600 \text{ seconds} = 360{,}000 \text{ joules}. \tag{4}$$

Although this number is correct, it's kind of inconvenient to keep multiplying everything by 3600, so engineers came up with another measurement of energy, the "kilowatt hour." A kilowatt is 1000 watts (kilo is the SI prefix that means 1000). So the energy consumed by our 100 watt lightbulb over 1 hour could also be denoted as

$$100 \frac{\text{joule}}{\text{second}} \times 1 \text{ hour } \times \frac{1 \text{ kW}}{1000 \text{ J/s}} = 0.1 \text{ kW-hr}. \tag{5}$$

This is exactly the same amount of energy as 360,000 joules, just expressed in a different unit. It's kind of a funny unit: a kilowatt-hour is "energy per second times hours." If we did the same thing for volumetric flow rate, we might say "gallons per minute times hours," which of course is simply some number of gallons. Despite being an odd unit, the kW-hr is widely used because it's convenient for expressing energy consumption on an hour timescale.

In regard to coffee, the primary focus for us here is transferring electrical energy to heat energy. When you plug in an electric hot water kettle, the energy of the moving electrons is transferred to heat through a "resistive element." Essentially, the moving electrons generate some heat each time they collide with a molecule inside the resistor that doesn't allow them to move so easily. The higher the electrical current (i.e., how many electrons per second), the more collisions occur, and more energy is transferred to heat.

How much actual energy is required to heat the water? A key physical concept is that every kind of matter has a "specific heat capacity," which is defined as the amount of energy required to raise 1 gram by 1 degree Celsius. If we denote the specific heat capacity as C_p, then the energy required to heat a given mass m of some material by a temperature difference $\Delta T = T_{final} - T_{initial}$ is

$$\text{Energy} = m \times C_p \times \Delta T. \tag{6}$$

Hopefully this expression is intuitive. (Check the units on the right hand side of the equation and make sure after multiplying through you have units of energy.) If you try to heat a larger mass, more energy is needed; if you try to raise the temperature by a lot, then more energy is needed. Precisely how much energy depends on the specific heat capacity of that material, which varies with the chemical composition of the material. Many metals (like copper or gold) have pretty low specific heat capacities, around 0.3. Water actually has a very large specific heat capacity, around 4.2 J/(g × °C), which means a large amount of energy is required to heat it up. You don't have to take our word for it, however: you'll be measuring C_p for water yourself in this lab.

Part A – The Energy to Heat Water

1) First, review the instructions on use of the electric water kettle for heating water, and set the kettle for 95°C. Don't start it yet!

2) Add a known mass of water to the kettle (about half full); make sure you record the mass of water! Plug in the kettle through a zeroed Kill-a-Watt meter, but still don't turn it on yet.

3) On the next page, you will record the time, the water temperature, and the cumulative kW-hrs of energy.

4) Once you're all set, turn on the kettle, and begin recording the instantaneous water temperature and time, about every 20 to 30 seconds. Every time the energy reading of the Kill-a-Watt meter increases by 0.01 kW-hr, record the temperature and the time.

5) Discard the hot water, and repeat the measurements one more time. Use a different mass of water, with the kettle almost full (record this new mass). Make sure you zero your Kill-a-Watt meter and let the temperature settle before turning on the kettle (the water will heat up a bit as the kettle is hot). Again, once you are set, record the time, temperature and energy at every change in 0.01 kW-hr. Later you will graph and analyze these data, but discuss with your lab mates – qualitatively how does the energy usage vary with temperature and time?

6) Don't discard the full kettle of hot water – you're going to use that water in part B.

Temperature vs. Time Data

Mass of water in **HALF-FULL** kettle: _____ *grams*

Time (sec)	Temp. (°C)	Energy (kW-hr)	Time (sec)	Temp. (°C)	Energy (kW-hr)
_____	_____	_____	_____	_____	_____
_____	_____	_____	_____	_____	_____
_____	_____	_____	_____	_____	_____
_____	_____	_____	_____	_____	_____
_____	_____	_____	_____	_____	_____
_____	_____	_____	_____	_____	_____
_____	_____	_____	_____	_____	_____
_____	_____	_____	_____	_____	_____
_____	_____	_____	_____	_____	_____
_____	_____	_____	_____	_____	_____

Temperature vs. Time Data (continued)

Mass of water in **ALMOST-FULL** kettle: _____ *grams*

Time (sec)	Temp. (°C)	Energy (kW-hr)	Time (sec)	Temp. (°C)	Energy (kW-hr)

Part B – Taste Comparisons of Light and Dark Roasts

1) Set the electric kettle to the side momentarily. It is now time to use the Clever Coffee Dripper, again, for two head-to-head brews… but this time both will be your own roasts from Lab 3.

2) Set up two Clever Coffee Drippers to brew. You will be doing a taste comparison, so try your best to prepare the beans from the two roasts identically: grind equal masses, and try to grind them equivalently (so the particulates are similar in size).

3) For at least one of your roasts, use the meter to measure the energy usage of grinding. Put in a known mass of roasted coffee beans to grind. You can't measure the energy directly in kW-hr, since the grinder uses so little energy. You can estimate it, however, using the Kill-a-Watt meter's instantaneous measure of the power (in Watts) being drawn by the device. The key hint is that the meters also measure the instantaneous electrical power… and what do you multiply electrical power by to get energy?

4) Decide the brew ratio and water temperature you will use, estimate the grind size (better yet take a picture in the grinder to start keeping track of the grind), and decide on an extraction time. Brew and make sure you have correctly recorded all the pertinent data.

Energy Data for Grinder

Mass of roasted beans: _____ *grams*

Power output during grinding: _____ *Watts (or Joules/second)*

Time spent grinding: _____ *seconds*

Energy usage: _____ × _____ = _____ *Joules*

Energy usage in kW-hr: _____ × _____ = _____ *kW-hr*

5) Now, time for a blind taste test! Have one person in your group be the server, and have the other(s) turn around and/or close their eyes. Serve out samples to your lab mates into two different small cups, but don't let them know which is which. Taste each one. Can you determine which is your light roast and which is your dark roast? Refer to the coffee flavor wheel – what flavor notes do you detect? Which one tastes "best"? Write down your sensory impressions of each brew.

Data for Brewing Blind Taste Test

Grind size: _____   Water temperature: _____ °C

Mass of hot water: _____ *grams*   Mass of beans: _____ *grams* R_{brew}: _____

Extraction time: _____ *minutes*

Coffee type and Roast level: _____

Sensory Evaluations / Blind tasting notes:

_____

_____

_____

Coffee type and Roast level: _____

Sensory Evaluations / Blind tasting notes:

_____

_____

_____

Special warnings about hot air popcorn roasters
1) Don't put in too much or too little – you need about 65 to 75 grams.
2) As soon as you turn it on, immediately check to make sure the beans are swirling… if not, you will start a fire!
3) A damp paper towel in a bowl is a good way to catch the chaff.

Part C – The Energy of Roasting

1) The next activity is to roast some beans using your "Air Crazy" roaster. You will do this twice – once to get a feel for the roasting process and once where you measure temperature and energy consumption as a function of roast time. Do not roast for longer than 8 minutes; these roasters typically cannot get hot enough to yield a dark roast. A time of 5 minutes usually yields a good light city roast. During the roast, keep track of time and carefully note when you hear the "first crack". **Stop your roast about 1 minute after first crack starts!** Also note the color of the roast, the kW-hr, etc. During the second roast, you will measure the temperature and energy consumption. Record the mass of the green beans and resulting roasted beans.

2) To do the first roast, add green beans to a bit above the air vents in the roaster, approximately 65-75 grams. Record the volume of the green beans. The amount of beans can be varied, but there are rules of thumb; too much and the beans will not be "fluidized" sufficiently leading to an uneven roast; too few and some will actually fly out of the popper. Typically, when you first turn on the "Air Crazy" roaster, the mass of beans should be moving slowly. As the roast continues, the beans become less dense and move more rapidly.

3) To catch the chaff, direct the outflow of the "Air Crazy" towards a wet paper towel in a bowl. At all times be extremely careful – the roaster and all plastic and metal parts become very hot during the roasting process.

4) Dump the roasted beans into the metal colander to cool. Record their mass, then bag and label (after they're cool!) to taste in next week's lab.

5) During the second roast, repeat the process but measure and record the temperature and the energy consumption (in kW-hrs) every 20 seconds for the duration of the roast. (Reset the Kill-a-watt before you start!) Be even more careful not to burn yourself when you are measuring the temperature in the roaster. The thermocouple will become very hot, greater than 200°C. Use the oven mitts when handling all parts of the roaster. Record the volume and masses of the green beans and roasted beans.

6) Perform one more roast, but use the Nesco. Remember that the minimum mass of green beans in the Nesco is 100 grams (compared to about 65 grams in the Air Crazy). Determine the energy usage as well for this roast. Measure the mass of green beans and roasted beans. You will be comparing the energy usage of the two roasters on a "per gram" basis, i.e., how many kW-hr used per gram of green beans.

Energy Data with Hot Air Popcorn Roaster

1st roast Coffee type: _____

Mass of green beans: _____ *grams*

Mass of roasted beans: _____ *grams*

Time of first crack: _____ *minutes*

Time spent roasting: _____ *minutes*   Energy usage: _____ *kW-hr*

2nd roast Coffee type: _____

Mass of green beans: _____ *grams*   Mass of roasted beans: _____ *grams*

Time of first crack: _____ *minutes*

Time spent roasting: _____ *minutes*   Energy usage: _____ *kW-hr*

Time (sec)	Temp. (°C)	Energy (kW-hr)	Time (sec)	Temp. (°C)	Energy (kW-hr)
_____	_____	_____	_____	_____	_____
_____	_____	_____	_____	_____	_____
_____	_____	_____	_____	_____	_____
_____	_____	_____	_____	_____	_____
_____	_____	_____	_____	_____	_____
_____	_____	_____	_____	_____	_____
_____	_____	_____	_____	_____	_____
_____	_____	_____	_____	_____	_____
_____	_____	_____	_____	_____	_____
_____	_____	_____	_____	_____	_____

Energy Data with Nesco

3rd roast Coffee type: _____

Mass of green beans: _____ *grams*   Mass of roasted beans: _____ *grams*

Time of first crack: _____ *minutes*   (might be hard to hear!)

Time spent roasting: _____ *minutes*   Energy usage: _____ *kW-hr*

Lab Report

By your specified due date, each group will submit their lab report that includes the following: (1) two scatter plots for heating water: temperature vs. time, and temperature vs. energy; (2) a spreadsheet table of your C_p calculations for water; (3) a scatter plot of your roasting temperature profile and energy usage; (4) a column plot showing the energy per mass for each unit operation; and (5) brief paragraphs discussing your observations.

(1) Enter your electric water kettle data (the time/energy/temperature measurements) into Excel, and prepare the following three scatter plots: (i) temperature vs. time, (ii) cumulative energy (in kW-hr) vs. time, and (iii) cumulative energy versus temperature. Make sure you use good practices in spreadsheet analysis – put axes labels on each graph! Each of the three scatter plots will have two distinct curves, for both of the two masses of water that you heated. Make sure each scatter plot has a legend that specifies which set of points corresponds to which mass of water. What trends do you observe?

(2) Next, prepare a table in Excel that has 4 columns: mass, overall ΔT, overall total energy, and C_p. Here "overall" refers to the change between the beginning and end of the trial. Enter the two sets of data (one for each mass), and then calculate C_p in the fourth column using an appropriate formula. (Which is what? Examine equation 6...) Report your measured heat capacity in terms of $J/(g \times °C)$. How closely do your calculated values correspond to the established specific heat capacity for water?

(3) Now, for the roasting. Prepare a plot of your roast profile, i.e., your temperature versus time, for the hot-air roaster. Also prepare a plot of the energy (in kW-hr) versus time.

(4) Prepare a column chart that compares the energy usage for the four different pieces of equipment you measured: the kettle, the hot air roaster, the Nesco roaster, and the grinder. Important: each of these pieces of equipment works on a different mass of material, so normalize your energy usage on a mass basis. In other words, calculate how much energy per gram of water for the kettle, how much energy per gram of green coffee beans for the roasters, and how much energy per gram of roasted coffee for the grinder. Make sure your column plot is clearly labeled.

(5) On a final separate page, write clear answers the following questions using no more than a few sentences each:

(i) What trends do you see in your temperature & energy measurements versus time for heating water? How did your measured specific heat capacity for water compare to the established value? Be quantitative – what percent difference is there? What might account for any discrepancy?

(ii) What qualitative impressions (tasting notes) did you have about the light roast compared to the dark roast? How did the brews prepared in the Clever Coffee Dripper compare to those you've made previously in the Mr. Coffee?

(iii) At what time and temperature did first crack occur? Add any additional notes on how the roast color changed as a function of time.

(iv) During roasting, why did the temperature and energy usage vary in time in the fashion you observed? What effect did you think it had on the chemical reactions occurring during roasting?

(v) Which roaster used "more" energy? Think carefully about this: which roaster used more energy per mass of green beans?

Lab 4 Bonus Box – Water: The Fluid of Life (and Coffee)

Water: the fluid of life? Yes, water is pretty unique, and frankly special. Water is one of the most important fluids on the planet – and the universe. First, and most obviously, we couldn't survive without water. In the context of coffee, water is almost 99% of what we are drinking in the cup. But that is just the starting point for why water is so interesting.

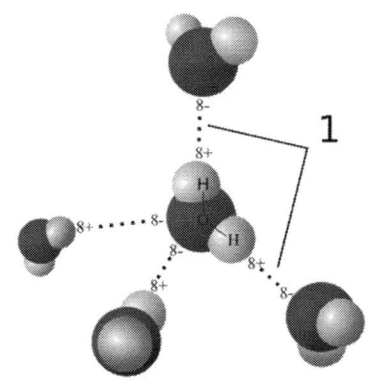

In terms of its chemical structure, water is H_2O – two hydrogen atoms bonded to an oxygen atom. The figure at right shows the sort of structure or orientation of water molecules relative to each other in ice, where the dark sphere represents oxygen and the lighter spheres are the hydrogens. Because oxygen has what's known as "lone pair electrons" and is very "electronegative" (which simply means that it attracts electrons), each water molecule can form "hydrogen bonds" with surrounding water molecules (as depicted by the dashed lines). All the details of this are pretty cool, but the main aspect of this (if you aren't interested in the details) is that water forms hydrogen bonds with itself and consequently has structure. Why do we care? Well, because of this structure, when you freeze water the molecules are able to make those hydrogen bonds really well – so that each water molecule is hydrogen bonded to 4 other water molecules – and they, therefore, make a nice crystal structure. This ordered crystal formation is why we have the beauty of snowflakes like the one shown here.

In liquid water, the molecules can move around more so there are actually less than 4 hydrogen bonds per water molecule. As a result, the water molecules can actually be a little closer. These differences in packing are why ice floats on liquid water – ice is less dense than liquid water because the hydrogen bonds keep the molecules a little further apart on average. The lower density of ice also means that the water actually expands upon freezing. Most liquids contract or decrease in volume when they freeze or solidify. Pretty cool, but a note of caution – this is why you shouldn't freeze water in a sealed bottle or container. If you put a can of soda in the freezer, the can will bulge and potentially burst, leaving a slushy mess.

In terms of life, ice being less dense than liquid water is pretty important if you think about bodies of water like oceans or lakes. If ice were denser than liquid water, lakes would freeze from the bottom and then continue freezing all the way up, killing the plant life and beaching the animal life on a giant, solid ice cube; less plants, less fish, less animals, less life.

Another interesting point regarding the need for each water molecule in ice to make 4 hydrogen bonds is that this can't happen at the very surface of ice. At the surface there isn't water surrounding all of the molecules, but air on one side. Air can't hydrogen bond. Because of this, the surface molecules of water are not as strongly bound and are fluid, which enables you to ski, snow board, and ice skate. The slipperiness of that thin liquid water layer at the surface enables your skies, board, or skates to easily slide due to the fact that you are actually skidding along liquid water. In fact, the surface layer of ice doesn't actually freeze until about -10°C or 14°F. At this point you actually are on solid ice and the friction goes up dramatically. Of course, not too many people are interested in trying to ski, snow board, or skate when it's that cold (brrrrr!)

These changes from solid to liquid are captured in the "phase diagram" of water, which tells you at what temperature and pressure water is in its various phases like solid (ice), liquid (water), and gas (vapor). The large arrow shows what happens at 1 atmosphere (that's normal atmospheric pressure at sea level). The horizontal dashed line is 1 atmosphere pressure and the vertical lines show the melting or freezing point and the boiling point of water. As you move horizontally to the right along that

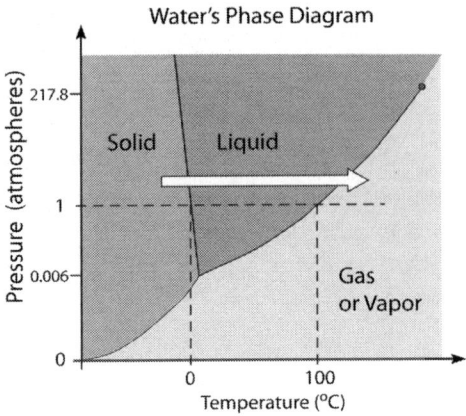

dashed line, below 0°C, water is in the form of ice, as you heat and move to the right the water melts at 0°C turning into liquid water, and if you keep heating it will start to boil at 100°C.

If you like to go hiking up in the mountains, you might have noticed some differences when you cook. A big reason for these changes can be understood from the phase diagram of water. As you go up in elevation, atmospheric pressure decreases – that's what makes it harder to breath. At an elevation of 8000 feet (1.5 miles above sea level) the pressure is only about 0.75 atmospheres, or 25% lower than the pressure at sea level. Now, if you look back at our phase diagram, the lower pressure means that water actually freezes at a slightly higher temperature and water boils at a lower temperature - about 92°C instead of 100°C. That's why you have to cook pasta longer when you are backpacking (the boiling water is not as hot up there), and the instructions for baking a cake are different at high elevations vs. at sea level.

How does this matter for coffee? Well, another cool thing is that below a certain pressure – around 0.006 atmospheres, which you can reach pretty easily reach with a vacuum pump – when you heat ice it doesn't actually melt to a liquid. Instead, it goes directly from the solid phase to the gas phase. This process of going from a solid directly to a gas is called "sublimation," and is easy to observe with dry ice (made of solid frozen carbon dioxide). If a material (like coffee) has water in it, then the sublimation process removes the water without melting it. You can freeze the coffee then put it under vacuum, sucking all the moisture out as water vapor. This "freeze drying" process is used not only to make instant coffee but also to process and store various pharmaceuticals that would degrade if they were left in liquid water. Almost half of the instant coffee sold in the United States is freeze dried. Spray drying is used for the rest where small coffee droplets are sprayed and allowed to come in contact with heated air to evaporate the water. Freeze drying is a little more expensive than spray drying but is thought to better preserve the aroma and flavor molecules. To make both methods more economical, the brewed coffee is first concentrated using a variety of techniques before drying.

Many coffee aficionados look down on instant coffee, and it is true that instant coffee is not that popular in the United States. Around the world, however, instant coffee is actually about 40% of the global coffee market – which is a lot of coffee, made possible by the phase diagram of water!

Lab 5 – Mass Transfer and "Flux" in Brewing

Objectives: In this lab we will study the concepts of mass transfer and flux as applied to the extraction of solid coffee grounds into water. We will compare quantitative measurements of "total dissolved solids" with qualitative sensory evaluations of the taste.

Equipment:

☐ Clever Coffee Drippers ☐ Electric kettle ☐ Digital refractometer

☐ Kill-a-Watt meter ☐ Roaster ☐ Paper cups

Activities:

☐ Part A – measuring TDS and PE with several Clever Coffee brews

  ☐ Three brews at different grind sizes

  ☐ Two brews at different temperatures

  ☐ Two brews, with periodic samples to get TDS vs. extraction time

☐ Part B – one or two roasts to have beans for next time

Report:

☐ Labeled column plot of TDS vs. brew condition

☐ Labeled column plot of PE vs. brew condition

☐ Scatter plot of TDS vs. extraction time

☐ Paragraphs discussing tasting notes and key questions about the lab

Background – Mass Transfer

In chemical engineering, a crucial question one often has to consider is "How do we get the chemicals from over here to over there?" This question applies at large length scales (such as in large pipelines), but even more importantly at small molecular length scales. This consideration can be seen very clearly in the case of coffee. Getting the organic flavor molecules and caffeine from the solid coffee grounds into to the hot water is a pivotal step that often determines the overall quality of the brewed coffee.

In this lab, we will consider two key ideas in regard to mass transfer at the molecular scale. The first is the idea of "flux," which to engineers has a very specific meaning:

$$\text{Flux} = \text{"amount of stuff" per unit area per unit time} = \frac{\text{moles}}{\text{m}^2 \times \text{s}} \quad (1)$$

The flux is thus a measure of how much stuff (i.e., how many moles of molecules) are moving through a particular area per unit time. If, as is often the case, you are interested in how many total molecules have transferred, you would integrate over the total area and the total time. With regard to coffee, this concept thus has two key implications: (1) The more surface area of the solid particulates, the more area you have for flux, the more molecules you'll get, and (2) the longer you expose it for, the more molecules you'll get. In the lab, we will directly compare grind size and extraction time on how much "coffee stuff" you extract into the water during brewing.

The second key idea is that the magnitude of the flux is proportional to the "concentration difference." One representation of this famous observation is

$$\text{Flux} = k \times (C_s - C_b). \quad (2)$$

Here C_s is the concentration of some molecule (say caffeine) at the surface of the solid particulates (coffee grounds), while C_b is the concentration of that molecule in the bulk of the fluid further away from the solid. The parameter k is known as a "mass transfer coefficient" and is a measure of how easily a molecule can move around. Big molecules are slow and cumbersome, while small molecules bounce around quickly. Importantly, k depends on temperature: the higher the temperature, the higher the mass transfer coefficient. Furthermore, k depends on whether the molecules get any help moving around because the liquid itself is moving. If you stir the mixture, then k is larger and you get a higher flux.

The concentration difference $(C_s - C_b)$ provides the "driving force" for mass transfer. You'll get the highest driving force, and hence the highest flux, if the concentration in the water (C_b) is initially zero. As time progresses, C_s decreases (because the molecules in the solid particles are being depleted), while C_b increases. Eventually the water is saturated with the molecule and you won't get any more mass transfer (because $C_s = C_b$). This is why it's usually a terrible idea to use already brewed coffee to extract from fresh grounds: all you're doing is extracting the few remaining bitter molecules that weren't fully extracted the first time around.

Background – Brew Strength & Extraction

What do you do if you brew coffee that is too "weak" or too "strong"? We intuitively know that if the brew is too strong we should increase the brew ratio or grind the coffee beans a little coarser. If you have a brewing method where you control the time for brewing, you might decrease the extraction time. This laboratory will provide a fundamental understanding of mass transfer and why these sorts of adjustments dramatically alter the quality and "strength" of the brew. Because there are so many different types of molecules in brewed coffee, it is challenging to measure the concentration of any specific molecule. Instead, we measure the cumulative concentration of *all* the different molecules that move from the solid coffee grounds to the liquid. This cumulative concentration is known as the Total Dissolved Solids (TDS), and is often expressed as a mass percentage. In brewed coffee, a typical TDS is about 1%, which means that 1% by mass is dissolved solids, and close to 99% is water (with the remainder as trace emulsified oils and gasses).

Usually when people refer qualitatively to how "strong" a particular cup of coffee is, they are responding to their perception of the TDS. It is easy to visualize that 'weak,' mostly translucent coffee has a relatively small TDS, while 'strong', extremely dark coffee has a large TDS. This perspective, however, is incomplete. A second independent variable governing the quality of the brew is the "percent extraction" (PE), which refers to the percent weight of solids originally in the coffee grounds that were transferred to the liquid phase. (The PE is also known as the "yield" or "extraction yield.") In other words, the PE is how much of the solid coffee mass is <u>removed</u> from the grounds to the water. Typical coffee grounds are composed of about 70% cellulose and other compounds that simply won't dissolve in water. The maximum possible PE is thus about 30%.

It is undesirable, however, to extract all 30% of the soluble compounds. Taste tests have consistently found that coffee extracted to the full 30% is unpleasantly bitter. In contrast, 'under-extracted' coffee at less than about 15% PE is unpleasantly sour and vegetal. The broad consensus is that coffee should be extracted to within the range 18% < PE < 22%.

How do you measure the PE? There is no easy way of directly measuring PE, but you can calculate it indirectly using the same sort of mass balance that we discussed in Lab 2. The main idea is the same: the mass of coffee molecules fed into a unit operation must be equal to the mass of coffee molecules that exits the unit operation, i.e.,

$$Mass\ of\ Coffee\ Solids\ In = Mass\ of\ Coffee\ Solids\ Out. \tag{3}$$

Recognizing that we have one stream of coffee solids moving in, but two streams that contain solids moving out, equation (3) means we have

$$m_{dry\ grounds} = m_{spent\ grounds} + m_{coffee\ solids\ in\ brew}. \tag{4}$$

We emphasize that each of the terms in equation 4 represents the mass of solids in that stream, so $m_{coffee\ solids\ in\ brew}$ is just the mass of solids in the brew, while $m_{spent\ grounds}$ represents *just* the mass of solids remaining in the spent grounds (*not* the combined mass of water and solids in the spent grounds). We can obtain the mass of coffee solids in the brew by measuring the TDS, so equation 4 becomes

$$m_{dry\ grounds} = m_{spent\ grounds} + \frac{TDS}{100} \times m_{brew}. \tag{5}$$

Note that because *TDS* is usually expressed as a percentage, we divide by 100 to make it a mass fraction.

Next, the percent extraction is defined as "how much of the original solids were removed into the liquid," so we have

$$m_{spent\ grounds} = \left(1 - \frac{PE}{100}\right) \times m_{dry\ grounds}. \tag{6}$$

Substitution of equation (5) into equation (4) and rearrangement yields our final expression,

$$PE = TDS \times \frac{m_{brew}}{m_{dry\ grounds}}. \tag{7}$$

Hopefully this result is intuitive: the higher the TDS in the brew, the higher the extraction from the solid phase must have been. The important point is that measurement of the brew TDS, along with weighing the dry grounds and the brew, gives an estimate of the percent extraction – and a useful measure of whether you are under- or over-extracting your coffee.

Part A – Exploration of Mass Transfer & Extraction

Our primary experiments today will focus on comparing different mass transfer or extraction protocols to assess their effects on the final taste and amount of "coffee stuff" extracted into the brew. We will use the Clever Coffee drippers to set up several extraction tests. For each brew we will measure the TDS in the brewed coffee with a digital refractometer, calculate the corresponding PE, and perform sensory evaluations.

0) First, measure the TDS of plain tap water. A normal reading will be somewhere around 0.01% to about 0.05% (compared to coffee, which is around 1.25%). Repeat at least two more times during the lab session. One reason to do this is to get a standard deviation, i.e., a measure of reproducibility. Another reason is to make sure that the refractometer is still calibrated properly and that the sample well isn't dirty.

1) Next, perform three simultaneous brews in the Clever Coffee Drippers to assess the impact of **Surface Area**. Use the same brew ratio, water temperature (~94°C), and extraction time (4 to 5 min), and compare 3 different grind sizes:

    i. Coarsely ground (as coarse as you can make it, or even whole bean if you like)
    ii. Medium ground (a 'normal' grind)
    iii. Finely ground (as fine as you can make it)

Make sure you do a taste of each brew, and that you get the mass of the brewed coffee as well as the TDS measurements. You will need both to calculate the PE.

2) The next goal is to assess the impact of **Temperature.** Perform two more brews, using the same brew ratio and extraction time as before, and a medium grind size. Compare two different temperatures:

    i. Moderate temperature (~70 °C)
    ii. Very hot temperature (around 99 °C).

Again, make sure you measure both the mass of the final brew and the TDS. Be careful when you taste the very hot one!

3) The final goal is to quantify the effect of **Extraction Time**. Prepare two more brews, again using the same brew ratio, medium grind size, and ~94°C temperature. Compare two different extraction times:

    i. Short time (1 minute)
    ii. Long time (10 minutes, with small samples every minute)

For the ten-minute trial, dispense a very small sample into a paper cup or Eppendorf one every minute. Before you dispense, give the contents of the Clever Coffee a gentle stir to mix everything up, and then dispense only a very small amount (enough to get a TDS reading in the refractometer). As before, weigh the mass of the brews, and taste.

PROPER USAGE OF THE REFRACTOMETERS

- **Let the coffee cool!** The meters will give error messages at high T. To cool it quickly, pipette a little bit into a paper cup, let it cool off for a few minutes, then pipette just a bit into the sample well of the refractometer.
- Only pipette enough to cover the glass sensor - don't add too much.
- Don't push the "menu" button... you don't need to change any settings.
- After you're done use a Kimwipe to clean the sensor.
- Don't move the refractometers... please be patient and wait for your turn.

TDS Data for Impact of Surface Area

Coffee type _____

Mass of hot water: _____ *grams*   Mass of grounds: _____ *grams* R_{brew}: _____

Temperature of hot water: _____ °C   Extraction time: _____ *minutes*

Grind size: **COARSE**

Mass of empty cup: _____ *grams*   Mass of filled cup: _____ *grams*

Mass of brew: _____ − _____ = _____ *grams*

TDS: _____ %   PE: _____ × _____ ÷ _____ = _____ %
                       TDS m_{brew} $m_{grounds}$

Sensory Evaluations:
_____
_____

Grind size: **MEDIUM**

Mass of empty cup: _____ *grams*   Mass of filled cup: _____ *grams*

Mass of brew: _____ − _____ = _____ *grams*

TDS: _____ %   PE: _____ × _____ ÷ _____ = _____ %

Sensory Evaluations:
_____
_____

Grind size: **FINE**

Mass of empty cup: _____ *grams*   Mass of filled cup: _____ *grams*

Mass of brew: _____ − _____ = _____ *grams*

TDS: _____ %   PE: _____ × _____ ÷ _____ = _____ %

Sensory Evaluations:
_____
_____

TDS Data for Plain Water

1st measurement: _____ %   2nd measurement: _____ %   3rd measurement: _____ %

TDS Data for Impact of Temperature

Coffee type _____

Mass of hot water: _____ *grams*   Mass of grounds: _____ *grams* R_{brew}: _____

Grind type: _____   Extraction time: _____ *minutes*

Temperature: <u>MODERATE TEMPERATURE</u>

Temperature of water: _____ °C

Mass of empty cup: _____ *grams*   Mass of filled cup: _____ *grams*

Mass of brew: _____ − _____ = _____ *grams*

TDS: _____ %   PE: _____ × _____ ÷ _____ = _____ %

Sensory Evaluations:
_____
_____
_____

Temperature: <u>VERY HOT</u>

Temperature of hot water: _____ °C

Mass of empty cup: _____ *grams*   Mass of filled cup: _____ *grams*

Mass of brew: _____ − _____ = _____ *grams*

TDS: _____ %   PE: _____ × _____ ÷ _____ = _____ %

Sensory Evaluations:
_____
_____
_____

TDS Data for Impact of Extraction Time

Coffee type_____

Mass of hot water: _____ *grams*   Mass of grounds: _____ *grams* R_{brew}:_____

Grind type: _____   Temperature of hot water: _____ °C

Extraction Time: **VERY SHORT**

Extraction time: _____ *minutes*

Mass of empty cup: _____ *grams*   Mass of filled cup: _____ *grams*

Mass of brew: _____ − _____ = _____ *grams*

TDS: _____ %   PE: _____ × _____ ÷ _____ = _____ %

Sensory Evaluations:

_____

_____

_____

Extraction Time: **VERY LONG**   (see also next page)

Extraction time: _____ *minutes*

Mass of empty cup: _____ *grams*   Mass of filled cup: _____ *grams*

Mass of brew: _____ − _____ = _____ *grams*

TDS: _____ %   PE: _____ × _____ ÷ _____ = _____ %

Sensory Evaluations:

_____

_____

_____

TDS versus Extraction Time

Time (minutes)	TDS	Time (minutes)	TDS
_____	_____	_____	_____
_____	_____	_____	_____
_____	_____	_____	_____
_____	_____	_____	_____
_____	_____	_____	_____
_____	_____	_____	_____
_____	_____	_____	_____

Part B – Roasting

Do two roasts for next time so that you have fresh beans ready to brew. Try different beans and roast levels to try to optimize the roast level for your beans.

Roasting Data

Coffee type: _____

Mass of green beans: _____ *grams*   Mass of roasted beans: _____ *grams*

Time spent roasting: _____ *minutes*   Energy usage: _____ *kW-hr*

Coffee type: _____

Mass of green beans: _____ *grams*   Mass of roasted beans: _____ *grams*

Time spent roasting: _____ *minutes*   Energy usage: _____ *kW-hr*

Lab Report

Each group will submit (1) a labeled column chart that shows the TDS value for each of your 7 brews, (2) a labeled column chart that shows the PE for each of your 7 brews, (3) a scatter plot of TDS vs. extraction time, and (4) a paragraph answering the questions below. On the column plots each column should be properly labeled, and you can use "insert text" to put some abbreviated tasting notes next to each column. (Choose one chart or the other to put the tasting notes on.) Then, on a separate page answer the following questions:

(1) What is the TDS of tap water? Do you think the number you obtained is reasonable? Why or why not? What is the TDS in PPM? (See the Lab 4 bonus box.)

(2) Which variable (grind size, temperature, or extraction time) had the most pronounced effect on TDS? Why do you think this was the case? (Hint: see equation 1.) Did it also have the most pronounced effect on qualitative taste? If not, why not?

(3) Likewise, which variable (grind size, temperature, or extraction time) had the most pronounced effect on PE? Did you see any differences in trends with PE when compared to the trends in TDS? If so, what might account for these differences?

(4) Recall the ideal extraction is typically considered to be about 20%, with a TDS near 1.3%. Which of your brewing conditions yielded a brew closest to those ideals? Did you think this was the best tasting coffee you brewed? How did it taste compared to the others? (Remember that the best measuring device for coffee taste isn't the TDS meter... it's your palate!)

(5) Describe how the TDS varied with extraction time. Why do you think it behaved like this? Do you think you would have obtained different results if you hadn't stirred the coffee before dispensing the small samples? What do you think would have happened to the TDS and PE if you let it brew for 20 minutes?

Lab 5 Bonus Box – What the Heck is "ppm"?

When the concentration of something is really, really small, one of the units that might be used is "parts per million," or ppm. For example, the amounts of certain naturally occurring chemicals in drinking water that are desirable (like sodium, magnesium, fluoride) or undesirable (like lead and arsenic) are often listed in ppm. Most cities issue water quality reports if you are interested in what your tap water contains. If you use tap water for your coffee brewing, then ultimately your coffee also has those chemicals!

Liquid	Approximate Dissolved solids
Distilled water	1 ppm
Bottled water	250 ppm
"Hard" tap water	450 ppm
Brackish water	3,000 ppm
Black coffee	13,000 ppm
Sea water	35,000 ppm

For example, in Davis, California the average level of sodium is 85 ppm, chloride is 21 ppm, and fluoride is 0.3 ppm. Some levels are so low that parts per billion (ppb) are used, like for lead which is less than 5 ppb.

So what exactly does ppm mean? If we use fluoride (F) as an example, 0.3 ppm means that there are 0.3 grams of fluoride per 1,000,000 grams of tap water. The units of measure here are grams, but any unit of measure can be used as long as they are the same for both quantities – like pounds or kilograms.

$$1 \text{ ppm F} = \frac{1 \text{ gram of F}}{1{,}000{,}000 \text{ grams of water}}, \text{ or in general, } 1 \text{ ppm} = \frac{1 \text{ unit of stuff}}{1{,}000{,}000 \text{ units of water}}$$

Fluoride is interesting because unlike Davis, most cities and towns supplement their water with fluoride to reach the level of 0.7 ppm recommended by the federal government's Health and Human Services Department. This is the recommended level to help prevent dental tooth decay. Too much fluoride in your water, however, results in dental fluorosis – a permanent change in the appearance of the tooth enamel from white spots in mild forms to staining or even pitting in severe cases. Fortunately, dental fluorosis is only really a concern when your teeth are developing, but that is the reason for all those lectures when you were young to spit out the tooth paste after brushing and rinse your mouth, as swallowing all that tooth paste day after day could lead to excess fluoride and dental fluorosis.

But what do ppm and different chemicals in water have to do with coffee? Well, coffee contains a cornucopia of different chemical molecules extracted from the roasted coffee beans in the ppm level. When you are measuring TDS to quantify all of the stuff in the brewed coffee, the ideal is around 1.3% TDS, which if you convert to ppm is

$$1.3\% \text{ TDS} = \frac{1.3 \text{ grams of solids}}{100 \text{ grams of water}} = \frac{1.3 \text{ grams of solids}}{10^6 \text{ grams of water}} \times \frac{10^6 \text{ grams of water}}{100 \text{ grams of water}} = \frac{13{,}000 \text{ grams of solids}}{10^6 \text{ grams of water}} = 13{,}000 \text{ ppm}.$$

That might sound like a lot, but many of the individual and important flavor molecules are in the 10 to 100 ppm range or lower (remember there are about 1000 different molecules that contribute to the flavor of coffee!) The low levels of all sorts of different chemicals in the coffee is part of what makes it so darn difficult to optimize brewed coffee through chemical analysis. The myriad of chemical reactions that occur during roasting are too complex to fully analyze, and the low concentrations makes it hard to quantify their effect on the brew's taste profile. Moreover, people's sensitivity to the various flavor molecules varies. Add the fact that the chemical content of the starting water is also variable based on the water source, and all in all the analysis and optimization of coffee becomes a very difficult scientific problem. Of course, you should use all the analytical tools you have available, but at the end of the day, the best measuring devices are your own taste buds.

Lab 6 – Coffee as a Colloidal Fluid & the Effect of Filtration

Objectives: In this lab we will study two important concepts. First, we will study fluid mechanics as applied to the motion of water through coffee grounds. Second, we will examine the "colloidal particles" in the coffee using optical microscopy, and assess how the filtration method affects the quantity of colloids and the mouthfeel of the coffee.

Equipment:

☐ AeroPress ☐ French press ☐ Metal filter ☐ Electric kettle

☐ Digital refractometer ☐ Kill-a-Watt meter ☐ Roaster ☐ Microscope

Activities:

☐ Part A – four brews with the AeroPress, to examine Darcy's law

☐ Part B – probing the effect of filtration

   ☐ Two AeroPress brews, comparing paper and metal filters

   ☐ One French press brew

   ☐ Microscope observations to see the brew colloids and oil droplets

☐ Part C – one or two roasts to have beans for next time

Report:

☐ Scatter plot of TDS versus extraction time

☐ Column plot of TDS for different filtration methods

☐ Description of microscopy observations

☐ Paragraphs discussing tasting notes and key questions about the lab

Background – Fluid Mechanics

We have learned in previous labs that the "extraction time" is a critical parameter that affects the final taste of the coffee: too short of a time yields sour and "under-extracted" coffee, but too long of a time yields bitter and "over-extracted" coffee. In most methods of brewing coffee, the extraction time is controlled by how quickly the hot water moves past the coffee grounds. In other words, the fluid velocity is a key parameter, so understanding 'fluid mechanics' is necessary.

The motion of fluids, like all other forms of matter, is governed by Newton's second law, i.e., $F = ma$ (where F is the sum of the forces acting on the fluid, m is the mass, and a is the acceleration). Unlike the rigid objects (like cannonballs etc.) you might have studied previously in physics courses, a key difference for fluids is that

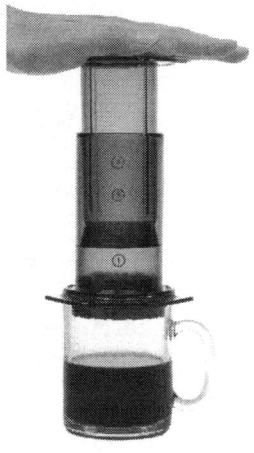

they are deformable. This difference tremendously complicates interpretation of the forces acting on fluids, so there are entire courses in engineering curricula dedicated just to fluid mechanics.

For the purpose of this lab, we will focus on how liquids move through "porous media," in this case coffee grounds. Specifically, there is an empirical equation known as Darcy's Law which states that the velocity v of the liquid (in cm/s) is proportional to the pressure difference across the porous medium:

$$v \sim \frac{\kappa}{\mu} \times \nabla P = \frac{\kappa}{\mu} \times \frac{(P_{entrance} - P_{exit})}{L}. \qquad (1)$$

There are several terms here, so let's define them. The "viscosity" μ of the fluid characterizes how easy it is for it to deform or to "shear". Water has a low viscosity, whereas honey has a very high viscosity. The "permeability" κ characterizes how much open space there is in the porous medium versus solid surface area: the higher the surface area to volume ratio, the more surface area is available to "slow" down the fluid. As a result, finely ground coffee has a higher surface-area-to-volume ratio and smaller permeability than coarsely ground coffee. (Think of a single, whole Rubik's cube representing a coarsely ground coffee particle vs. each small cube of the Rubik's cube as a separate element, where each individual element is a finely ground particle). The surface-area-to-volume ratio is also a great way to think about how grind level affected flux in Lab 5 – there is much larger surface area with smaller particle sizes so the rate of mass transfer is much faster.

Finally, the pressure gradient ∇P is the "driving force" for the fluid flow. (Recall that pressure is force/area.) Note that the "gradient" in pressure is how much the pressure changes over the length L of the porous medium. When you use the Mr. Coffee or a pour-over technique, the pressure difference is provided by gravity acting on the weight of the water. Other devices, however, provide more control over the pressure gradient (most famously in espresso machines). A key goal today is to gain a qualitative appreciation for Darcy's law and how quickly fluid flows through the porous coffee grounds and affects the taste of the resulting cup. The lower the applied pressure, the longer the effective extraction time will be – with a corresponding impact on the mass transfer and ultimate sensory qualities of the brew.

Background – Colloidal Particles and Filtration

In Lab 5 we talked about the "Total Dissolved Solids" in the brew. By "dissolved," we mean that each individual molecule is surrounded by water molecules. Not all of the mass that is extracted from the grounds, however, are dissolved organic molecules. There are three other types of matter extracted from the solid grounds and in the brew that you drink.

First, there are dissolved gasses, primarily carbon dioxide and VOCs. The concentration of CO_2 is especially high in freshly roasted beans (because the CO_2 hasn't had sufficient time to leak away). When you pour hot water over grounds that have a large enough amount of CO_2 still in them, you'll actually see bubbles rising up to the top of the slurry. This is exactly the same type of bubble formation and flotation that happens with beer or soda, except that the CO_2 concentration isn't as high in coffee. Nonetheless the bubble formation is a good indication that you're dealing with freshly roasted coffee.

Second, some amount of "non-dissolved solids" makes it past the filter and into the brew. Ideally during grinding you would make coffee particles all of the same size, but this never happens. Instead there is a distribution of sizes, with some larger particles, many intermediate particles, and some very small ones. Any particles smaller than the average pore size in the filter are carried into the brew for you to consume. These small particles are referred to as "colloidal particles," where colloidal is the scientific term that simply means "microscopically dispersed and insoluble." Colloids are typically in the range of 1 to 10,000 nanometers (i.e., up to about 10 microns). A key characteristic of colloids is that they undergo "Brownian motion." This is the same sort of random jiggling motion that individual molecules perform, but some colloids are large enough that you can see the Brownian motion with a standard optical microscope. In coffee, the colloids strongly affect the "body" (the mouthfeel) by altering the viscosity of the brew. The more colloids, the more viscous and higher the "mouth feel".

Third, there are "emulsified oils" in the brew. The term "emulsion" simply means a colloidal suspension made of liquid droplets rather than solid; the classic example is oil-in-vinegar salad dressing. Roasting coffee releases a variety of oils, which are especially evident in very dark roasts. As with the solid colloids, the emulsified oil droplets also affect the mouthfeel by altering the viscosity. The oil drops tend to be more 'potent,' however, because many of the more bitter tasting molecules tend to be more oil soluble than water soluble – which means the oil drops tend to impart a more bitter flavor to the brew. Typically a little bit of oil is desired for good mouthfeel, but not too much for bitterness.

Both the colloids and the emulsified oil are strongly affected by the type of filtration. The average size of the pores in the filter directly control the size of the colloids that make it into your brew. If you use a very coarse filter with big pores, obviously you let more colloids into your brew. Less obvious is that the composition of the filter also matters tremendously. Paper filters are made of cellulosic fibers, and cellulose is both hydrophobic (water-fearing) and oleophilic (oil-loving). In other words, paper filters will preferentially absorb the emulsified oil, so that little of it ends up in your brew. In contrast, metal filters are more oleophobic. They will let the oil droplets pass through uninterrupted.

Part A – Fluid Mechanics & the AeroPress

We will perform four brews using the AeroPress to get a qualitative feel for Darcy's law. Last week we saw how varying the grind size changed the surface area to volume ratio and hence the rate of mass transfer into the liquid. Here we will see that the grind size also affects the permeability and hence the "residence time," or the amount of time the hot water contacts the coffee grounds. The second set of experiments will be at constant grind size but at different pressure gradients using the AeroPress. In each case we will measure the time required for the water to move through the grounds.

1) We will do three initial trials all at the same grind size. Prepare enough ground coffee for three brews in the Aeropress (about 50 grams of coffee). Use the standard paper fil-

PROPER USAGE OF THE AEROPRESS

Be careful with the AeroPress – it is easy to burn yourself if careless!
- The maximum capacity is about 200 grams of water.
- Make sure the filter holder is hand-tight and secure. If it is loose, the brew can fall out onto your hand and burn you badly. If it is crooked, brew will leak out the side.
- Hold it steady with one hand as you apply an evenly applied pressure straight down. Avoid pushing it a little sideways.
- Don't forget the filter paper or metallic filter – otherwise the brew will rush out, and you'll get a gritty mess.

ters for all trials in Part A.

2) For the first trial, put the coffee grounds inside the AeroPress, set up a cell phone timer, and then add the hot water. Give a quick stir, and wait 4 minutes to provide some extraction time. At the four-minute mark, for this first trial apply a very "gentle" continuous pressure. Measure the "dispensing time," i.e., how long it takes you to push the plunger to the bottom.

3) Measure the TDS, and taste the brew. What are your sensory impressions?

4) For the second trial, repeat the process with everything identical but apply a "strong" continuous pressure, and repeat the measurements. The time required to dispense the fluid should decrease when you increase your applied pressure.

5) For the third trial, double the mass of coffee, so that the height of the coffee grounds in the AeroPress is doubled (i.e., L is doubled). Apply the same "gentle" continuous pressure, and repeat the measurements. Again, what changes do you observe?

6) For the fourth and final AeroPress trial, use a very coarse grind size. (This is tantamount to increasing the effective permeability of the porous medium.) Try to apply the same "gentle" continuous pressure as the previous trial, and repeat the measurements. Again, what changes do you observe?

Part B – Colloids and Filtration

We will perform four more brews, focusing on the effect of filtration on the colloids and emulsified oils that end up in the brew. We will also do some optical microscopy to see what the coffee colloids look like.

1) First, set up two AeroPresses with identical conditions (same grind size, same mass of coffee same mass of water), except use a paper filter in one and a metallic filter in the other. Perform the brew with the same extraction time and same pressure.

2) Measure the TDS of each, and taste the brews. What are your sensory impressions? Can you detect a difference in body / mouthfeel? Oils tend to accumulate at the surface of your brew (because oil is less dense than water)... can you see any oil?

3) Set up a small French press, and try to use identical conditions as you used with the AeroPress (same brew ratio, same grind size). At the four minute mark use the press to filter out the grounds and dispense the coffee. Measure the TDS and taste the brew – how does it compare to the AeroPress?

4) Next, let's do some microscopy. Prepare a microscope slide by pipetting out a bit of coffee from your French press brew, and take a look at it in the microscope. Can you identify the coffee colloids? Do you see any oil droplets? (The colloids will be

PROPER USAGE OF THE REFRACTOMETERS

Be aware that the presence of any large particulates or oil droplets in your sample on the refractometer will give rise to large errors in the reading (because the relatively large objects alter the light path). Pipette your coffee from near the top of your sample, not the bottom! Avoid putting samples with visible particulates or oil films, and make sure the refractometer is cleaned before you measure your sample.

irregular, oil droplets will be spherical.) Approximately how large are they? Do you see any evidence of Brownian motion? If possible on your microscope, take some images of the things that you find in the brew.

5) Also use the microscope to examine one of your more filtered brews. What differences do you observe?

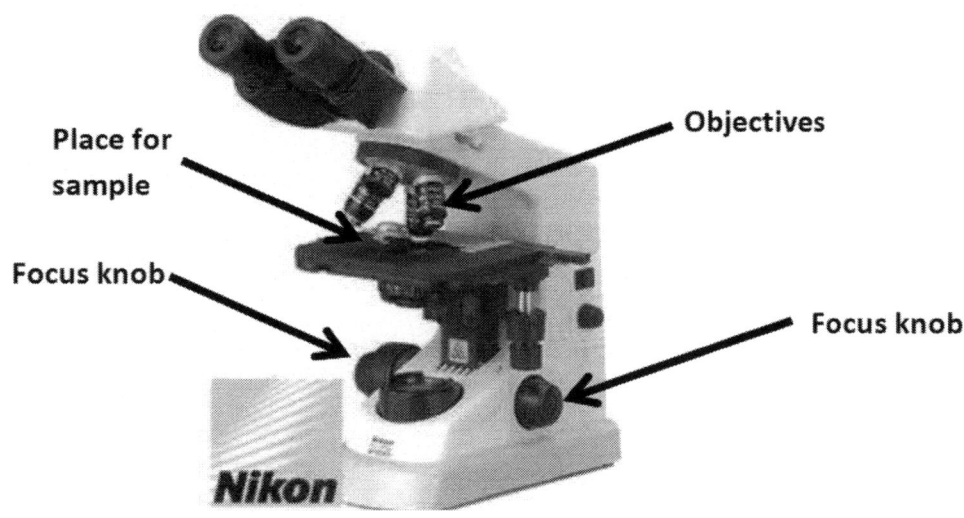

Part C - Roasting

Finally, do two or more roasts for next time. Keep track of your energy usage! The remaining laboratory experiments will focus on the design competition, so optimizing roasting will be a critical aspect. Have you found a roast level for the available green beans that you like?

Data for Fluid Mechanics Experiments – Comparing Pressure

Coffee type_____

Mass of hot water: _____ *grams*   Mass of grounds: _____ *grams* R_{brew}: _____

Temperature of hot water: _____ °C   Grind size: _____

Initial extraction time: _____ *minutes*

Brew Method: AeroPress, Gentle Pressure

Total extraction time after pressure applied: _____ *seconds*

Mass of empty cup: _____ *grams*   Mass of filled cup: _____ *grams*

Mass of brew: _____ – _____ = _____ *grams*

TDS: _____ %   PE: _____ × _____ ÷ _____ = _____ %

Sensory Evaluations:

_____

_____

_____

Brew Method: AeroPress, Strong Pressure

Total extraction time after pressure applied: _____ *seconds*

Mass of empty cup: _____ *grams*   Mass of filled cup: _____ *grams*

Mass of brew: _____ – _____ = _____ *grams*

TDS: _____ %   PE: _____ × _____ ÷ _____ = _____ %

Sensory Evaluations:

_____

_____

_____

Data for Fluid Mechanics Experiments – Comparing *L* and Permeability

Brew Method: <u>AeroPress, Gentle Pressure, Double Coffee Mass (Large *L*)</u>

Mass of hot water: _____ *grams*   Mass of grounds: _____ *grams* R_{brew}: _____

Total extraction time after pressure applied: _____ *seconds*

Mass of empty cup: _____ *grams*   Mass of filled cup: _____ *grams*

Mass of brew: _____ − _____ = _____ *grams*

TDS: _____ %   PE: _____ × _____ ÷ _____ = _____ %

Sensory Evaluations:
_____
_____
_____

Brew Method: <u>AeroPress, Gentle Pressure, Very Coarse Grind</u>

Grind size: _____

Total extraction time after pressure applied: _____ *seconds*

Mass of empty cup: _____ *grams*   Mass of filled cup: _____ *grams*

Mass of brew: _____ − _____ = _____ *grams*

TDS: _____ %   PE: _____ × _____ ÷ _____ = _____ %

Sensory Evaluations:
_____
_____
_____

Data for Colloidal Filtration Experiments – Comparing Filter Type

Coffee type_____

Mass of hot water: _____ *grams*   Mass of grounds: _____ *grams* R_{brew}: _____

Temperature of hot water: _____ °C   Grind size: _____

Initial extraction time: _____ *minutes*

Brew Method: AeroPress, Paper Filter

Mass of empty cup: _____ *grams*   Mass of filled cup: _____ *grams*

Mass of brew: _____ − _____ = _____ *grams*

TDS: _____ %   PE: _____ × _____ ÷ _____ = _____ %

Sensory Evaluations:

_____

_____

_____

_____

Brew Method: AeroPress, Metal Filter

Mass of empty cup: _____ *grams*   Mass of filled cup: _____ *grams*

Mass of brew: _____ − _____ = _____ *grams*

TDS: _____ %   PE: _____ × _____ ÷ _____ = _____ %

Sensory Evaluations:

_____

_____

_____

_____

Microscopy Observations

Brew sample: _____

Observations and Notes:

_____

_____

_____

_____

Brew sample: _____

Observations and Notes:

_____

_____

_____

_____

Roasting Data

Coffee type: _____

Mass of green beans: _____ *grams*   Mass of roasted beans: _____ *grams*

Time spent roasting: _____ *minutes*   Energy usage: _____ *kW-hr*

Coffee type: _____

Mass of green beans: _____ *grams*   Mass of roasted beans: _____ *grams*

Time spent roasting: _____ *minutes*   Energy usage: _____ *kW-hr*

Roasting Data (continued)

Coffee type: _____

Mass of green beans: _____ *grams*   Mass of roasted beans: _____ *grams*

Time spent roasting: _____ *minutes*   Energy usage: _____ *kW-hr*

Coffee type: _____

Mass of green beans: _____ *grams*   Mass of roasted beans: _____ *grams*

Time spent roasting: _____ *minutes*   Energy usage: _____ *kW-hr*

Lab Report

Each group will submit a report with the following material.

(1) A scatter plot that shows the TDS versus your measured dispensing times for the AeroPress. There should be at least 4 data points (from the AeroPress). Insert text boxes near each point to identify what grind size and pressure you used. Make sure you label your axes.

(2) A column plot that shows the TDS versus your filtration method. Clearly label each column. What trends do you observe?

(3) A brief paragraph answering the following questions:

  (i) How significantly did the applied pressure affect the rate at which fluid moved through the grounds by gravity? How did this affect the TDS and taste? Was there any effect on PE?

  (ii) How did the increased amount of grounds (doubled L) affect the rate at which fluid moved through the grounds in the AeroPress? How did the grind size affect the rate? How did this affect the TDS and taste? Was there any effect on PE?

  (iii) Discuss your group's observations about the effect of filtration on the TDS and PE of your brews, as well as the corresponding sensory evaluations. Also describe your group's observations of the coffee samples under the microscope.

Lab 6 Bonus Box – Why is Coffee Filtered?

Do you have a favorite coffee brewing method? From an automatic drip, to the French press, AeroPress, Chemex, vacuum brewers, to old-school percolators and even espresso makers – all of these brewing methods have some sort of filtration. But, **why** do we filter the brew – is it just to keep the sludge from the bottom of your cup? Or is there more to it than that?

First, let's start by thinking about "cowboy coffee" – yes, that is the formal name for throwing some coarsely ground coffee into water, heating it (usually over a campfire) and then pouring the brew into a cup for consumption. At this point you might already be worried about drinking cowboy coffee and have an inkling as to why it is known to either put hair on your chest (or remove the hair you already have). The reason for cowboy coffee's bad reputation is twofold: the uncontrolled extraction, and the difficulty in controlling the heat so that the coffee isn't boiled. Recall Lab 3: leaving the coffee heating on the campfire further degrades the quality through those chemical reactions that decrease pH.

Even if you were able to control the temperature on the campfire, you'll still have difficulty controlling the extraction. Recall our ideal brew is 18-22% extraction. Since 26-30% of the mass of a roasted coffee bean is extractable, that means we are leaving some of the extractable coffee stuff behind. The idea behind this is that different flavor components have different solubilities in water, and those last few percent that take longer to extract are associated with bitter characteristics – thus some of the hair-growing (or removing) capabilities of cowboy coffee. Over extracting is avoided by filtering which stops the extraction (i.e., ends the contact time) simply by removing the grounds. Most coffee aficionados identify a 91 to 94°C brewing temperature as ideal for limiting the extraction of "bitter" flavor compounds, so most brewing methods and extraction times are based on this temperature range. Of course, temperature matters greatly because it alters solubility. If you ever made sugar crystals as a kid, you know that the solubility of sugar goes up tremendously (by a factor of 3) when you heat water from room temperature to 100°C. Allow the sugar water to cool, and you can make sugar crystals on a string because the sugar becomes less soluble and must come out of solution (crystallize or precipitate) as it cools.

To make a much better cup of cowboy coffee, just heat the water first (if the water is brought to a boil, allow it to cool for a minute), then throw in the coffee. This will give you much better control over the water temperature and the extraction. After 4-6 minutes, simply pour yourself and the other "cowboys or cowgirls" a cup of pretty good brew. You can even use the lid of the pot to keep most of the grinds out of your cup, which could be considered coarse filtration.

Another reason to filter your brew is to control the body or "mouth feel" of the brew. Mouth feel is the tactile sensation of the coffee in the mouth, and is highly related to the viscosity or how easily it flows. Some folks like a lot of body and should use a coarser filter (think large pores in a metal filter or French press), while others prefer a lighter mouth feel and should use a fine filter size. There is surprisingly little data in the open literature on the pore size of typical paper coffee filters, with unreferenced websites stating between 5 and 100 microns (0.1mm). This is a huge range. If you look at filter paper under a microscope like the image on the next page, you will see a range of various shaped pores with sizes from 5-30 microns, but it also depends on where you look and the manufacturer of the paper as to the typical pore size. Filter paper is composed of lignocellulosic fibrous material, which is simply wood pulp primarily from fast growing trees like bamboo. The paper is crêped so that the coffee can more easily flow through the layers of fibers. The filter paper also varies based on whether the filter is canonical or flat bottom in shape. Specialty Chemex filters are reportedly thicker with smaller pores. In comparison, metal or mesh filters are much more uniform as can be seen from the table and images on the right.

Filter Type	Pore Shape	Pore Size (microns)
Paper	woven	5-100
AeroPress Paper	woven	5-30
Aero Metal (Fine)	round	200
Aero Metal (Coarse)	round	250
Gold Tone Mesh	square	150
Nylon Mesh	square	250
French Press	rectangle	180-230

Differences in pore sizes and their density (i.e., percentage of surface area) affect the amount of ground coffee particles that make their way into your cup as well as the water draining rate with gravity brewing methods. A typical automatic drip method usually uses 500-800 micron ground coffee particles. However, even when using a nice cone and burr grinder, you end up with a range of coffee particle sizes from about 10 microns to almost 1000 microns (where 1000 microns = 1 mm). This is also a huge range! It is analogous to grade distributions on an exam where the mean grade might be a "B", but all grades are represented across the class. The more uniform the grind size, the more uniform the extraction. Because of the coarser filtration and leakage around the sides of the filter with the French press, a typical grind size for this method is 600 – 1000 microns. In comparison, espresso grinds are around 200 microns, and Turkish coffee is more of a powder at 100 microns.

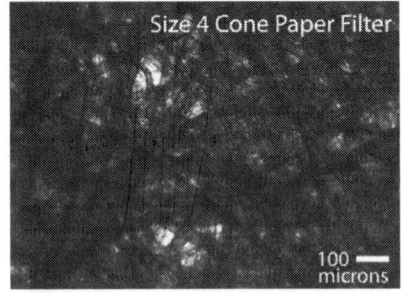

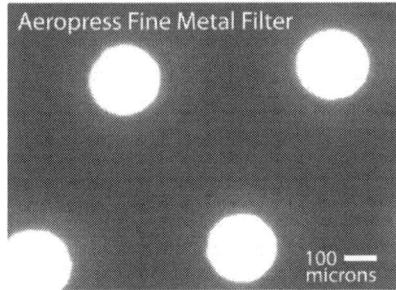

Another big difference between the filter types is the amount of oil from the ground coffee that makes its way into your cup. The highest amount of oil gets through with metal filters. Filter paper both adsorbs and absorbs the oil. Adsorption refers to the oil actually sticking to the paper fibers while absorption is the same phenomena as a sponge soaking up a liquid into the spaces of the sponge. If you look closely at coffee from an AeroPress with filter paper, you still get oil into the brewed coffee because the pressure you apply squeezes out a lot of the oil absorbed into the filter paper.

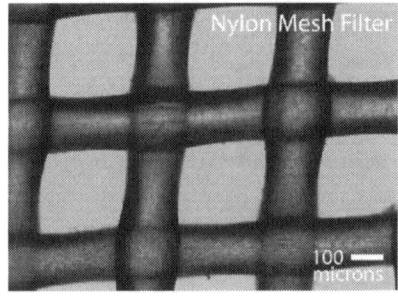

A final comment is that some coffee experts claim that you have to pre-wet your paper filter before you brew. Why would this be important? There are at least two possible reasons. First, some people can detect a "papery" flavor contributed by microscopic bits of paper that detach from the filter and make it into your brew. Pre-wetting washes these loose bits away. Second, if the filter paper is already fully wet, then it won't as easily absorb the first drips of coffee that might be packed with the most readily extractable flavor molecules. In other words, an initially dry filter paper will retain some of the initial drips of coffee, while a pre-wet filter won't. But does this matter? Do your own taste tests to find out!

Part II

Design of Coffee

Design Competition Format, Guidelines, & Video Project

The main goal of the coffee design project is to make the **best** cup of coffee, using the **least** amount of electrical energy. Each group will receive a score defined by the ratio

$$\text{Final Score} = \frac{\text{Blind Taste Test Score}}{\text{Total Electrical Energy}}$$

Note carefully what this metric implies: it is very possible for you to make the best tasting coffee, but to still lose the competition because your process used too much energy!

If there are sufficient people competing, then there are two rounds of competition. In the first round (the "playoffs"), groups will compete within their section. The group in each section that receives the highest final score will then advance to the second round (the "championship") to compete for the title of grand champion.

The two inputs into the final score are defined as follows.

- The coffee will be judged in a blind taste test on a scale of approximately –5 to 55 (where –5 is amazingly bad coffee, and 55 is stunningly good.) The point distribution is broadly based on the official tasting guidelines established by the Specialty Coffee Association of America (cf. Appendix D). All of the blind taste scores for each coffee will be averaged together.

- Your group must keep track of how many kilowatt-hours of electrical energy you used during the entire process of roasting and brewing your coffee. Your roasting energy will be "normalized" by how much mass of any particular roast you end up brewing. Your brewing energy, however, will not be normalized. Any piece of equipment you plug into an outlet must be monitored using the energy meter and included in your final tally. This is typically only the brewer or kettle and the roaster; as we saw in Lab 4 the energy of the grinder is negligible so we won't specifically keep track of it here.

In either round, groups who place in the top three in either taste score or taste per energy score will receive some bonus points, but only the winning group in terms of taste per energy will advance to the championship round. The group with the highest taste per energy score in the championship round will receive additional bonus points, as well as a grand prize. The bonus points are awarded to your laboratory report score as follows:

Playoff round	Taste Score	Final Score (Taste/Energy)
3rd place	+ 5	+ 5
2nd place	+ 10	+ 10
1st place	+ 15	+ 15

Championship round	Taste Score	Final Score (Taste/Energy)
3rd place	+ 5	+10
2nd place	+ 10	+20
1st place	+ 15	+30

The following design constraints must be followed.

1) **Ingredients:** The only ingredients you are allowed to use are green coffee beans and water. No syrups, sweeteners, spices, or other artificial flavors may be added.

2) **Minimum Volume:** For the play-off round, you must prepare enough for three dozen people to each get 1 fluid ounce taste of coffee. This means you must make at least 1oz x 36 people = 36 oz = 4.5 cups ≈ 1 liter of coffee. If your group makes it to the championship round, you must modify your design to make just 0.5 liters of coffee (because the championship blind tasting panel is assumed to be smaller).

3) **Energy Penalty:** If you don't deliver the minimum amount of required brew, you will be assessed an energy penalty of 0.002 kW-hr per gram of missing brew. (If you make more than the required amount, the energy penalty is zero.)

4) **Time Allowed:** On the day of the blind tasting, you will have 45 minutes to brew your 1 liter of coffee.

5) **Equipment:** You are free to use any combination of the equipment available in the lab for roasting and brewing your coffee.

6) **Cold Water:** You are only allowed to use regular cold **tap** water, not hot tap water, as your starting point for your brew. The kettles should be empty and cool to the touch before you start.

7) **No Flames:** Absolutely no open flames are allowed in the lab, so no portable stoves or burners.

8) **Negative Infinity:** Clever students will note that if their process uses *zero* electrical energy, then their final score will be infinity (because any tasting score divided by zero is infinity). One example of a zero electrical energy process would be to pour cold water over whole green beans. Although this is a clever idea in terms of energy minimization, note that *negative* tasting scores are possible (because of the 'balance' category). So it is likely that such a low energy process would actually get you in *last place* in regard to final score.

9) **Creativity:** Most importantly, remember that good engineers think of new ways of doing things... we encourage creative designs!

Final Design Project Video

Throughout the next three labs, you and your group will have time to work on making a video that presents your final design. The video must be less than 5 minutes, and must include the following material.

1) A process flow diagram that shows your unique process. There must be enough detail that somebody else can watch the video and replicate your process.

2) Your mass balances for water and solid (coffee). These can be shown on the process flow diagram. Make sure you include the waste streams!

3) Your type of roast(s). What beans did you use, and how did you roast them?

4) Your energy usages. Clearly describe the logic you followed to attempt to minimize energy costs.

5) Your TDS and PE for your one of your final design brews, or your competition brew from the contest. How close were you to the ostensible ideal range?

6) An overview of the sensory evaluations of your final brew as judged by the blind tasting.

7) A summary of anything you would do differently in a (hypothetical) future design contest to improve your coffee taste or minimize your energy usage.

Throughout the video there should be audio narration or text subtitles that help the viewer understand the information you're trying to convey. Pictures and video taken while you were roasting and brewing in lab are highly recommended but not strictly necessary.

You are free to use any software you like, as long as you include the required material. It is easy to download free movie editing software; we recommend "Microsoft Movie Maker" (versions 2.6 or above). You can use PowerPoint, PhotoShop, or any other program to make schematics, which can then be embedded in your video. All group members must help make the video, although nobody necessarily must appear personally in it. Make sure your names, section number, and date show up on a title screen near the beginning of your video. You can submit your video either directly as an MPG, or indirectly as a YouTube link.

Don't worry about having the perfect design yet – the next couple labs are intended for you to hone your roast and brew.

Lab 7 – First Design Trials: Optimizing Strength & Extraction

Objectives: The main goal of this lab is for you and your group to begin designing your process, with an emphasis on optimizing the strength and extraction of your brew.

Equipment:

☐ Brewer(s) ☐ Roaster(s) ☐ Digital refractometer ☐ Kill-a-Watt meter

Activities:

☐ At least three brews, completely quantified (TDS, PE, energy)

☐ At least two roasts, with energy measurements

Report:

☐ Data for three brews

☐ A completed energy scoresheet

☐ Comparison of predicted vs. calculated PE for one brew

☐ Paragraphs discussing tasting notes and proposed gameplan for next design trials

Background

If you think back on the first six labs, in each experiment we tried varying some experimental condition and then seeing what happened, with some insight provided by fundamental principles (e.g., conservation of mass). In other words, we were performing *analysis* of how the brewing method impacts coffee quality. Now we need to change our focus to *design*, where we use the knowledge gained via analysis to create a process that satisfies certain design goals.

In our case, we want to make the best-tasting coffee using the least amount of energy. As discussed back in Lab 5, a great deal of sensory analysis experiments have shown that people prefer the taste of coffee in a pretty narrow range of strength (TDS from about 1.2 to 1.45 %) and extraction (PE from about 18 to 22%). Refer to the graph below, which is a "coffee brewing control chart" that shows the different sensory evaluations one gets from brews prepared to different strengths and extractions. If your coffee tastes bitter, it is probably over-extracted (PE > 22%), but if it tastes sour or vegetal it is probably under-developed (PE < 18%). The TDS of the brew tends to amplify the intensity of the extracted flavors, inducing either "strong" or "weak" taste impressions.

Heretofore we made some coffee and then measured the TDS and PE after the fact. But what do we do if we want to predict these values *before* we do the experiment, i.e., if we want to design the process to yield coffee in the ideal range of TDS and PE?

To tackle this problem, we will combine several of our analytical results into a form that will be convenient for predicting the outcome of a brew. Recall that our mass balance on the coffee solids yielded an expression for the PE (equation 6 from lab 5),

$$PE = TDS \times \frac{m_{brew}}{m_{dry\ grounds}}. \qquad (1)$$

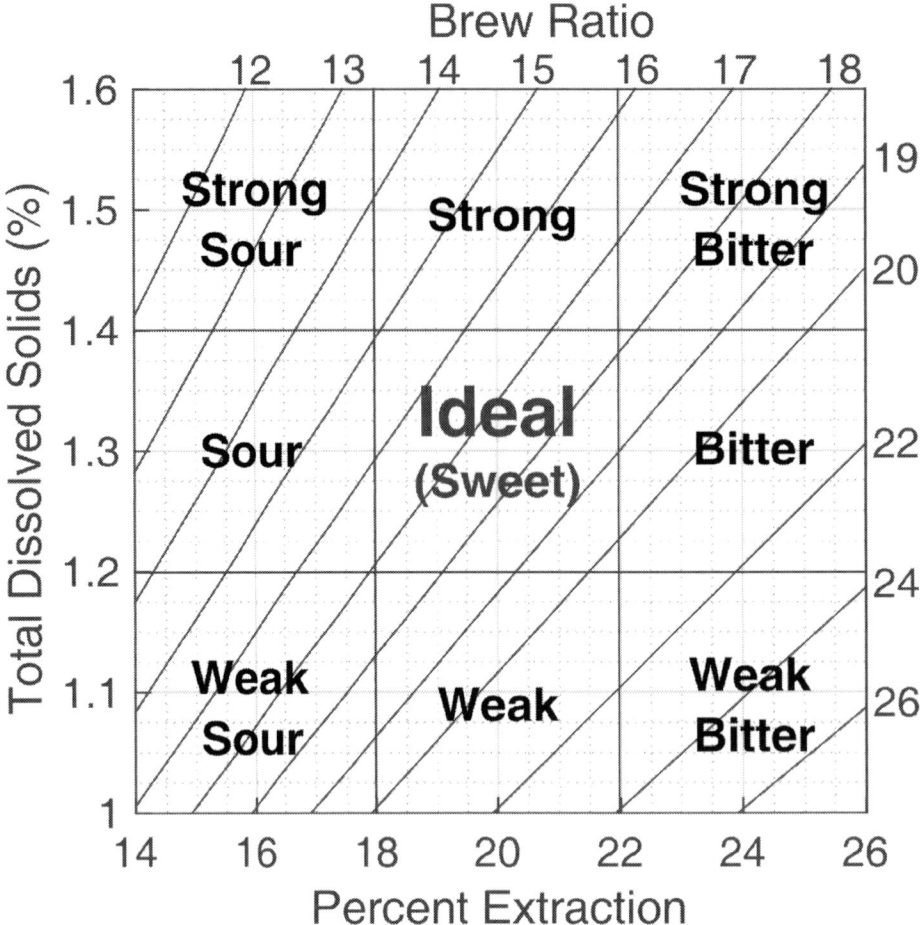

Also recall that our mass balance on the water yielded a prediction for the actual mass of the brew (equation 4 from lab 2),

$$m_{brew} = m_{feed} - (R_{abs} \times m_{dry\ grounds}). \qquad (2)$$

Substitution of our expression for m_{brew} into our expression for PE yields

$$PE = TDS \times (R_{brew} - R_{abs}), \qquad (3)$$

where recall R_{brew} is the "brew ratio" defined as the mass of hot water fed in over the mass of dry grounds, i.e., $R_{brew} = m_{feed}/m_{dry\ grounds}$. There is a hugely important design implication of equation 3: if you want to obtain a certain value of PE, you *cannot* independently choose a brew ratio and a TDS value. In other words, once you choose a brew ratio, there is only one possible TDS value that is consistent with the desired PE. This idea is captured in the diagonal lines superimposed on the coffee brewing control chart, which show the possible values of TDS and PE for the specified brew ratio. As you can see, there are only a narrow range of brew ratios that can yield brews within the ideal zone.

Once you choose a brew ratio, though, how do you specify the TDS? Again, the insights you gained via engineering analysis in the previous labs will now help you design the process. If your TDS (and hence PE) are too small and your brew is under-developed, then you likely had insufficient mass transfer during your extraction. This could be due to a grind that was too coarse, or an extraction time that was too short, or a water temperature that was too low. Likewise, if your TDS and PE are too large and your brew is bitter, you had too much transfer during your extraction: too fine a grind, too long an extraction time, or too high a water temperature. During your design trials today, don't try things randomly: use the insight you gained on mass transfer, as well as equation (3) above, to improve your brewed coffee.

Of course, don't forget that the quality of the brew depends on the quality of the chemical reactions that occurred during roasting. If you under- or over-roasted your beans, it won't matter how well you do the extraction, because you'll just be extracting out unpleasant tasting coffee. **You could extract black charcoal or Spanish roast beans to the 'ideal' range of 1.3% TDS and 20% PE... but it won't taste very good!** Remember as well, coffee beans are biological products that can vary from lot to lot. What worked for one type of beans last week won't necessarily work with a different type of beans this week. For example, the green beans might have different concentrations of sucrose depending on how they were grown, or perhaps they've been stored for different lengths of time and have degraded differently. Coffee is a moving target! You need to adjust your aim, i.e., refine your design, based on your experimental observations for any particular batch of beans.

Most importantly, your ultimate evaluation of brew quality should be based on your sensory evaluation of the taste. The TDS measuring devices are not perfect, so use all of the available information AND your perceived taste in your evaluation.

Summary of 1st Design Trial Activities

Unlike the previous labs, we intentionally leave the design trial activities open ended. Use the time to work with your group on making and testing your own process for roasting and brewing the best tasting coffee. You are welcome to use any combination of equipment available in the lab, and you can use the time as you think best. We urge you to think carefully, however, about the following questions.

1) What are the TDS and PE of your brews? Are they close to the ideal range? Do your own sensory evaluations accord with the taste descriptions on the coffee brewing control chart?

2) What is the best roasting procedure? Make sure you perform at least a couple roasts toward your ideal roast.

3) How much energy is each step using? Is your design energy efficient, or an energy hog? Make sure you get the required data to fill out the sample "energy scoring sheet," which is similar to what will be used in the design competition.

Data for 1st Design Trials

Coffee type_____

Roasting method: _____ Roasting date:_____

Mass of green beans: _____ *grams*   Mass of roasted beans: _____ *grams*

Time spent roasting: _____ *minutes*   Energy usage: _____ *kW-hr*

Brewing method: _____   Filtration method: _____

Mass of hot water: _____ *grams*   Mass of grounds: _____ *grams*   Ratio:_____

Water Temp: _____ °C   Energy usage: _____ *kW-hr*

Extraction time: _____ *minutes*   Grind size: _____

Mass of empty cup: _____ *grams*   Mass of filled cup: _____ *grams*

Mass of brew: _____ − _____ = _____ *grams*

TDS: _____ %   PE: _____ × _____ ÷ _____ = _____ %

Other data:

_____

_____

_____

Sensory Evaluations:

_____

_____

_____

_____

Data for 1st Design Trials

Coffee type_____

Roasting method: _____ Roasting date: _____

Mass of green beans: _____ *grams*   Mass of roasted beans: _____ *grams*

Time spent roasting: _____ *minutes*   Energy usage: _____ *kW-hr*

Brewing method: _____   Filtration method: _____

Mass of hot water: _____ *grams*   Mass of grounds: _____ *grams*   Ratio: _____

Water Temp: _____ °C   Energy usage: _____ *kW-hr*

Extraction time: _____ *minutes*   Grind size: _____

Mass of empty cup: _____ *grams*   Mass of filled cup: _____ *grams*

Mass of brew: _____ − _____ = _____ *grams*

TDS: _____ %   PE: _____ × _____ ÷ _____ = _____ %

Other data:
_____
_____
_____
_____

Sensory Evaluations:
_____
_____
_____
_____

Data for 1st Design Trials

Coffee type_____

Roasting method: _____ Roasting date: _____

Mass of green beans: _____ *grams*   Mass of roasted beans: _____ *grams*

Time spent roasting: _____ *minutes*   Energy usage: _____ *kW-hr*

Brewing method: _____   Filtration method: _____

Mass of hot water: _____ *grams*   Mass of grounds: _____ *grams*   Ratio: _____

Water Temp: _____ °C   Energy usage: _____ *kW-hr*

Extraction time: _____ *minutes*   Grind size: _____

Mass of empty cup: _____ *grams*   Mass of filled cup: _____ *grams*

Mass of brew: _____ − _____ = _____ *grams*

TDS: _____ %   PE: _____ × _____ ÷ _____ = _____ %

Other data:
_____
_____
_____
_____

Sensory Evaluations:
_____
_____
_____
_____

Data for 1st Design Trials

Coffee type _____

Roasting method: _____ Roasting date: _____

Mass of green beans: _____ *grams*   Mass of roasted beans: _____ *grams*

Time spent roasting: _____ *minutes*   Energy usage: _____ *kW-hr*

Brewing method: _____   Filtration method: _____

Mass of hot water: _____ *grams*   Mass of grounds: _____ *grams*   Ratio: _____

Water Temp: _____ °C   Energy usage: _____ *kW-hr*

Extraction time: _____ *minutes*   Grind size: _____

Mass of empty cup: _____ *grams*   Mass of filled cup: _____ *grams*

Mass of brew: _____ − _____ = _____ *grams*

TDS: _____ %   PE: _____ × _____ ÷ _____ = _____ %

Other data:

_____

_____

_____

Sensory Evaluations:

_____

_____

_____

_____

Sample Energy Scoring Sheet

If your brew uses beans from just one roast, then fill out only "Roast A" and put zero for "Roast B." If you use three or more roasts, append the data and calculate the total energy of roasting appropriately.

Roast A (bean type): _____   **Roast B** (bean type): _____

Mass of green beans: _____ *grams*   Mass of green beans: _____ *grams*

Mass of roasted beans: _____ *grams*   Mass of roasted beans: _____ *grams*

Energy to roast: _____ *kW-hr*   Energy to roast: _____ *kW-hr*

Energy to roast per gram roasted bean: Energy to roast per gram roasted bean:

_____ ÷ _____ = _____ *kW-hr/gram*   _____ ÷ _____ = _____ *kW-hr/gram*

Actual mass of beans used: _____ *grams*   Actual mass of beans used: _____ *grams*

Energy per gram × total grams used: Energy per gram × total grams used:

_____ × _____ = _____ *kW-hr*   _____ × _____ = _____ *kW-hr*

Total energy for roasted coffee actually used in brew (Roast A + Roast B):

_____ + _____ = _____ *kW-hr*

Total mass of water heated: _____ *grams*

Initial Water Temp: _____ °C   Final Water Temp: _____ °C

Energy used to heat water: _____ *kW-hr*

(Note: don't worry about the energy penalty now since you're not making a whole liter.)

Brewing method: _____

Mass of empty cup: _____ *grams*   Mass of filled cup: _____ *grams*

Mass of brew: _____ − _____ = _____ *grams*

If the brew mass is more than 975 grams (0.975 liter), **the energy penalty is zero.** Otherwise, calculate the energy penalty as follows:

Deficient mass: __975__ − _____ = _____ *grams*

Energy penalty: __NA__ *grams* × __0.002__ *kW-hr/gram* = __0__ *kW-hr*

Total energy used to produce your coffee (roast energy + water energy + penalty):

_____ + _____ + __0__ = _____ *kW-hr*

Roasting Data

Coffee type: _____

Mass of green beans: _____ *grams*   Mass of roasted beans: _____ *grams*

Time spent roasting: _____ *minutes*   Energy usage: _____ *kW-hr*

Coffee type: _____

Mass of green beans: _____ *grams*   Mass of roasted beans: _____ *grams*

Time spent roasting: _____ *minutes*   Energy usage: _____ *kW-hr*

Coffee type: _____

Mass of green beans: _____ *grams*   Mass of roasted beans: _____ *grams*

Time spent roasting: _____ *minutes*   Energy usage: _____ *kW-hr*

Coffee type: _____

Mass of green beans: _____ *grams*   Mass of roasted beans: _____ *grams*

Time spent roasting: _____ *minutes*   Energy usage: _____ *kW-hr*

Lab Report

By your specified due date, each group will submit a lab report that includes the following:

(1) For at least three brews, state (i) the brewing method, (ii) approximate grind level, (iii) TDS and PE, (iv) where the brew is on the control chart, and (v) tasting notes.

(2) A completed "energy scoring sheet" for whichever process you think is most promising for the competition. (A photo or scan of an energy score sheet is fine.)

(3) For at least one brew, a comparison of your measured PE using Equation 1 versus the PE predicted by equation (3)… how similar or dissimilar are the values?

(4) Finally, a paragraph that describes your main findings today, and a brief game plan for what you will test in your design next week. What logic or experimental data informed your design choices?

Lab 7 Bonus Box – How is Coffee Decaffeinated?

The Lab 1 Bonus Box was titled "Caffeine the Wonder Drug," but what if you don't want caffeine in your coffee? Some folks are extra sensitive to caffeine. Others might like to have an after dinner cup of coffee deliciousness, but find it difficult to sleep afterwards. Everyone has heard of decaffeinated coffee, but how do they actually remove it?

As we mentioned earlier, caffeine is a natural molecule made by *Coffea* plants as a defensive mechanism against insects. A lot of folks think that dark roasts have more caffeine than light roasts, but the amount of caffeine is really dictated by the bean – not the roast level. Caffeine is an alkaloid (a nitrogen containing compound) and it is pretty impervious to the roasting process, so a dark or light roast of the same beans has about the same caffeine content. The differences in the amount of caffeine in a typical brew are mainly due to the amount of caffeine that happened to be in the bean to begin with, and how efficiently you extracted it during the brewing process.

Green beans are always decaffeinated **before** roasting. The first step invariably involves steam. The solubility of caffeine in water is highly sensitive to temperature: at room temperature the solubility is about 2 grams per 100 grams water, but it increases dramatically to 66 grams per 100 grams boiling water. As a result, the first step in any decaffeination process is to "swell" the green coffee beans with steam. The beans actually increase in size about 50% during steaming. This opens up the pores in the beans, making the caffeine more accessible. The steaming also helps to solvate and mobilize the caffeine molecules.

After the steaming step, there are four main methods for decaffeinating coffee, which are separated into "solvent-based" processes using chemicals and "non-solvent based" processes using water. (Actually, strictly speaking all of them use solvents since technically water is a solvent as well… but even though water is a chemical, using the phrase "chemical free" is a matter of semantics that is important to many consumers.) In the direct solvent process, a liquid that has a high caffeine solubility but a lower "coffee stuff" solubility (everything else that isn't caffeine) is contacted with the steamed green coffee beans so that the caffeine is selectively dissolved (or "solubilized") into the solvent. The solvents used in modern processes are typically ethyl acetate or methylene chloride. If ethyl acetate is used, the process is often termed "natural decaffeination" because ethyl acetate is found in fruit and can also be obtained from fermentation of sugar cane; it is considered more "natural" than chemically synthesized methylene chloride (called dichloromethane in Europe). Despite the natural name, the ethyl acetate actually used in decaffeination is produced chemically because it is much cheaper to synthesize than trying to extract the chemical from fruit or produce it by fermenting sugar. Regardless, both ethyl acetate and methylene chloride are actually mildly toxic so you don't want them in your cup of coffee. Fortunately, only a few ppm of either solvent remains at the end of the decaffeination process, and essentially none remains after the beans are roasted.

To extract the caffeine, the steamed coffee beans are simply soaked in the solvent for about 10 hours, the solvent is removed, and the green decaffeinated beans are re-steamed to remove any residual solvent. This process is called a "direct solvent" method because the green beans directly contact the solvent. In the "indirect solvent" method, the green beans are steamed and soaked in water, and water is then separated from the beans and then mixed with the solvent to extract the caffeine. This procedure keeps the beans from touching the solvent directly, but also tends to cause more loss of flavor compounds.

To help address this problem, and to avoid use of chemical solvents, alternative approaches that "recycle" the water have been developed. One such non-solvent based approach is the "Swiss water process." Named because it was developed in Switzerland (not because it uses Swiss water!), in this process the green beans are soaked in near-boiling water to remove the caffeine, which also inadvertently removes other soluble flavor molecules. The water is collected and the caffeine is removed by filtering through "activated charcoal." The charcoal has a porosity (average hole size) that allows the flavor molecules to get through but traps the larger caffeine molecules. After removing the caffeine, the green coffee "flavored" water is reused to remove the caffeine from the next batch of green beans. The first batch of beans are "sacrificial beans" that help saturate the water with the important flavor molecules that come out in the hot water along with the caffeine. After the caffeine is removed by the charcoal, the second batch of beans "sees" a liquid that already has lots of flavor molecules, so there is little driving force for the molecules to leave the beans – except for the caffeine, which will rapidly solubilize into the caffeine-free water. Reusing the water in this fashion helps prevent the extraction from the next batch of beans to be processed and so on.

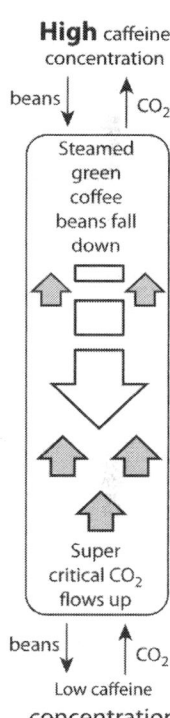

The fourth and final decaffeination technique involves something called "super critical carbon dioxide," which is some pretty interesting stuff. Carbon dioxide (CO_2) is a product of respiration – we exhale this gas as a by-product of using energy – and it is a product from reactions that burn or release energy (including coffee roasting). Caffeine and most other liquid and solid chemicals are not very soluble in CO_2 gas. However, if you compress CO_2 gas to a high enough pressure (around 250 atmospheres), it can remain in a sort of gas phase, but almost have the density of a liquid, which is why it has the moniker of "super critical." Even though caffeine isn't all that soluble in super critical CO_2, it is much more soluble that the other flavor molecules. After steaming the green beans, the wet, swelled-up beans are contacted with the super critical CO_2 in a "counter current" fashion: beans enter the top of the column and super critical CO_2 flows up from the bottom. As you learned in Lab 5, mass transfer depends on a concentration gradient. By having "fresh" CO_2 contact the already mostly caffeine extracted green beans that have been in contact with CO_2 since the top of the column, the concentration gradient can be enhanced over the length of the column to improve the caffeine transfer. The CO_2 is collected from the top of the tower and contacted with a water spray to leach the caffeine from the CO_2. The CO_2 is then recycled, while the nearly pure caffeine can be sold.

Having said all this, we should note that many folks believe that there simply is no such thing as a good cup of decaffeinated coffee. No matter what decaffeinating process is used, there is invariably some loss or degradation of the flavor molecules. The situation is improving, however. In the past much decaffeinated coffee was not that good to begin with – in other words, garbage in, garbage out. With modern techniques, and if you start with a high quality coffee and use careful processing, a cup of quality decaf can be produced.

Lab 8 – Second Design Trials: Scaling Up to One Liter of Coffee

Objectives: The main goal of this lab is to plan how to "scale up" your process efficiently to a larger volume, and to roast your beans for the competition!

Equipment:

☐ Brewer(s) ☐ Roaster(s) ☐ Digital refractometer ☐ Kill-a-Watt meter

Activities:

☐ At least three brews, completely quantified (TDS, PE, energy)

☐ At least two roasts, with energy measurements (for design competition)

☐ Consideration of time and energy usage

☐ Pictures and/or video as you desire for the final design video

Report:

☐ A completed energy scoresheet

☐ Estimates of how much water, coffee, energy, and time are needed for 1 liter

☐ Paragraphs discussing your proposed design and logic for design choices

Background

There are many processes that work beautifully at "small" scales, but are challenging (or impossible) to implement at "large" scales. For example, a chemist might devise an elegant chemical reaction process for synthesizing some desired compound. Even though the chemist can get the reaction to work in the lab, there might be many engineering challenges to overcome before the reaction process can be used industrially. If the reaction involves too many steps, or requires too many expensive catalysts, or only works at impractically high temperatures, or yields too many waste products, then we might conclude that the reaction can't be "scaled up" efficiently.

The same logic applies to coffee. Perhaps you have perfected a process for making a small cup of coffee that tastes great… but that doesn't necessarily mean you can use the same process to make a larger volume of coffee. Perhaps the process requires an unacceptably large amount of energy; perhaps the taste of the coffee changes when you try to brew over a larger volume; perhaps the process is so slow that it simply requires too much time.

The main goals of this design trial are (1) to roast the beans you will be using in the final competition and (2) to plan how to "scale up" your brewing process efficiently to a larger volume. It is crucial that you plan how much water, how much ground coffee, how much energy, and how much time are required. Don't waste time actually making a whole liter today – instead, optimize your design and plan how it will work!

Summary of 2nd Design Trial Activities

As with the first design trials, we intentionally leave the lab activities open-ended, so that you can work with your group on your own process design. This is also a great time to obtain some video for the video project if you so desire. We urge you to think carefully, however, about the following questions.

1) If you want to end up with 1 liter of brewed coffee, how much water will you need to heat? You don't want to waste energy heating up water that you don't use. You also don't want to end up short of a liter. Think back to Lab 2… what information do you need to plan a process yielding precisely 1 liter of coffee? Will the data you obtained in Lab 2 apply to your process? If not, what experiment could you do?

2) How can you predict how much energy will be required? (Remember Lab 4…)

3) Recall that you'll have 45 minutes to brew 1 liter of coffee. If your process involves any repeated slow steps, will you have sufficient time to make a whole liter? Contrariwise, if your process is really fast, will your brew be sitting around for a long time before anybody tastes it? (Recall your experience in Lab 3!) Note that some extra brewing equipment will be available for the competition.

4) Finally, make sure you bring your "A game" to your roast(s) for this lab… these are the beans you will be using in the design competition!

Make sure you measure the energy usage of each step. You will need the energy info to fill out a preliminary "energy sheet" like the one used during the actual competition. Also get the TDS and PE, but remember the TDS measuring devices are not perfect… your perceived taste evaluation is the most important criterion!

Roasting Data

Coffee type: _____

Mass of green beans: _____ *grams*   Mass of roasted beans: _____ *grams*

Time spent roasting: _____ *minutes*   Energy usage: _____ *kW-hr*

Coffee type: _____

Mass of green beans: _____ *grams*   Mass of roasted beans: _____ *grams*

Time spent roasting: _____ *minutes*   Energy usage: _____ *kW-hr*

Coffee type: _____

Mass of green beans: _____ *grams*   Mass of roasted beans: _____ *grams*

Time spent roasting: _____ *minutes*   Energy usage: _____ *kW-hr*

Coffee type: _____

Mass of green beans: _____ *grams*   Mass of roasted beans: _____ *grams*

Time spent roasting: _____ *minutes*   Energy usage: _____ *kW-hr*

Data for 2nd Design Trials

Coffee type _____

Roasting method: _____ Roasting date: _____

Mass of green beans: _____ *grams* Mass of roasted beans: _____ *grams*

Time spent roasting: _____ *minutes* Energy usage: _____ *kW-hr*

Brewing method: _____ Filtration method: _____

Mass of hot water: _____ *grams* Mass of grounds: _____ *grams* Ratio: _____

Water Temp: _____ °C Energy usage: _____ *kW-hr*

Extraction time: _____ *minutes* Grind size: _____

Mass of empty cup: _____ *grams* Mass of filled cup: _____ *grams*

Mass of brew: _____ − _____ = _____ *grams*

TDS: _____ % PE: _____ × _____ ÷ _____ = _____ %

Other data:
_____
_____
_____

Sensory Evaluations:
_____
_____
_____
_____

Data for 2nd Design Trials

Coffee type _____

Roasting method: _____ Roasting date: _____

Mass of green beans: _____ *grams*   Mass of roasted beans: _____ *grams*

Time spent roasting: _____ *minutes*   Energy usage: _____ *kW-hr*

Brewing method: _____   Filtration method: _____

Mass of hot water: _____ *grams*   Mass of grounds: _____ *grams*   Ratio: _____

Water Temp: _____ °C   Energy usage: _____ *kW-hr*

Extraction time: _____ *minutes*   Grind size: _____

Mass of empty cup: _____ *grams*   Mass of filled cup: _____ *grams*

Mass of brew: _____ − _____ = _____ *grams*

TDS: _____ %   PE: _____ × _____ ÷ _____ = _____ %

Other data:
_____
_____
_____

Sensory Evaluations:
_____
_____
_____

Data for 2nd Design Trials

Coffee type_____

Roasting method: _____ Roasting date: _____

Mass of green beans: _____ *grams* Mass of roasted beans: _____ *grams*

Time spent roasting: _____ *minutes* Energy usage: _____ *kW-hr*

Brewing method: _____ Filtration method: _____

Mass of hot water: _____ *grams* Mass of grounds: _____ *grams* Ratio: _____

Water Temp: _____ °C   Energy usage: _____ *kW-hr*

Extraction time: _____ *minutes* Grind size: _____

Mass of empty cup: _____ *grams* Mass of filled cup: _____ *grams*

Mass of brew: _____ − _____ = _____ *grams*

TDS: _____ %   PE: _____ × _____ ÷ _____ = _____ %

Other data:
_____
_____
_____
_____

Sensory Evaluations:
_____
_____
_____
_____

Sample Energy Scoring Sheet

If your brew uses beans from just one roast, then fill out only "Roast A" and put zero for "Roast B." If you use three or more roasts, append the data and calculate the total energy of roasting appropriately.

Roast A (bean type): _____   **Roast B** (bean type): _____

Mass of green beans: _____ *grams*   Mass of green beans: _____ *grams*

Mass of roasted beans: _____ *grams*   Mass of roasted beans: _____ *grams*

Energy to roast: _____ *kW-hr*   Energy to roast: _____ *kW-hr*

Energy to roast per gram roasted bean: Energy to roast per gram roasted bean:

_____ ÷ _____ = _____ *kW-hr/gram*   _____ ÷ _____ = _____ *kW-hr/gram*

Actual mass of beans used: _____ *grams*   Actual mass of beans used: _____ *grams*

Energy per gram × total grams used: Energy per gram × total grams used:

_____ × _____ = _____ *kW-hr*   _____ × _____ = _____ *kW-hr*

Total energy for roasted coffee actually used in brew (Roast A + Roast B):

_____ + _____ = _____ *kW-hr*

Total mass of water heated: _____ *grams*

Initial Water Temp: _____ °C   Final Water Temp: _____ °C

Energy used to heat water: _____ *kW-hr*

(Note: don't worry about the energy penalty now since you're not making a whole liter.)

Brewing method: _____

Mass of empty cup: _____ *grams*   Mass of filled cup: _____ *grams*

Mass of brew: _____ – _____ = _____ *grams*

If the brew mass is more than 975 grams (0.975 liter), the energy penalty is zero. Otherwise, calculate the energy penalty as follows:

Deficient mass: __975__ – _____ = _____ *grams*

Energy penalty: __N/A__ *grams* × __0.002__ *kW-hr/gram* = _____ *kW-hr*

Total energy used to produce your coffee (roast energy + water energy + penalty):

Lab Report

By your specified due date, each group will submit a lab report that includes the following:

(1) A completed "energy scoring sheet" for whichever process you think is most promising for the competition. (A photo or scan of an energy score sheet is fine.)

(2) An estimate of the total amount of water and ground coffee that you will need to make 1 liter of brewed coffee at the competition, along with a corresponding estimate of how much energy will be used. How much time will be required to brew a complete liter? Show all of your calculations (with units).

(3) A paragraph that describes the brewing method, roast information, approximate grind level, your TDS and PE, where you are on the ideal brewing chart, your tasting notes, and any other information you feel is relevant.

(4) Another paragraph that describes *why* you have selected your chosen process for the competition. What logic or data informed your design choices?

Lab 8 Bonus Box – How is instant coffee made?

In the United States we don't really think that much about instant coffee. Only a piddling 3% of the coffee consumed in the US is instant, a shockingly small amount given that Americans are well known to be willing to pay a premium for convenience and speed. In contrast, more than 1/3 of the coffee consumed worldwide is instant coffee. Moreover, the consumption of instant coffee is increasing rapidly – it has tripled over the past 15 years. The percentage of instant coffee sold in the US is close to the smallest in the world.

It's not that Americans don't drink coffee. The average American drinks 2.6 cups of coffee a day. Some of the discrepancy is due to the surge in coffee pods in the US. Those single servings of coffee that can be brewed with the push of a button now make up 25% of the American market. They are fast and convenient, but not "instant" coffee.

Anywhere else in the world, instant coffee has a huge footprint. Nestlé (also known as Nescafé) actually buys 15% of all the coffee produced each year. Although "instant" coffee was first reportedly developed around 1771 in Britain, it wasn't till 1938 that Nestlé developed a reasonably palatable version. During that time, Brazil was producing a large excess of coffee and the Brazilian government started an initiative to figure out what to do with the excess coffee. Nestlé came up with a method of drying coffee with carbohydrates that reportedly was drinkable. The timing was perfect. Shortly thereafter, the advent of World War II solidified the place of instant coffee as a quick and convenient method to fuel soldiers.

Today, instant coffee is made by two processes: spray drying or freeze drying. In spray drying, concentrated brewed coffee is sprayed to make a fine mist and dried with hot air. To concentrate the coffee, it is brewed at a high coffee to water ratio. Some of the water is then evaporated off to yield a 50% or greater strength. That's pretty concentrated as a typical cup of coffee has a concentration of about 1.3%. The concentrated mist is then sprayed at the top of a tower, and hot air is blown upwards from the bottom of the column (similar to the counter current flow for caffeine extraction in the Lab 7 Bonus Box). At the bottom of the column the dried coffee particles are collected. Those particles are agglomerated (stuck together with a little water) to make larger particles. Agglomeration is how they make instant coffee powder look more like ground coffee when you open the package. Once the particles have the size and look that the manufacturer wants, it's packaged and ready to go.

In freeze drying, the concentrated coffee is first frozen before drying. It sounds a little like iced coffee, but the starting point is coffee ice cubes. These cubes are broken into small pieces and then put into a vacuum chamber and dried. In the Lab 4 Bonus Box, the phase diagram of water is shown. As you may recall, at pressures below 0.006 atmospheres when you heat ice it doesn't actually melt but vaporizes – the water molecules go directly from the solid phase to the gas phase. This process is called sublimation or "freeze drying." Freeze drying costs quite a bit more than spray drying, but most high quality instant coffee manufacturers use freeze drying because this process retains more of the aroma and flavor molecules than spray drying, resulting in a better tasting instant brew. In fact, those volatile aroma and flavor molecules are so critical to the quality that there are even processes that collect the gases during the extraction (brewing) phase and evaporation phase to try to add them back into the instant coffee. A lot of work to make an instant drink!

Lab 9 – Design Competition & Blind Taste Panel

Objective: To obtain fame, glory, and bonus points by winning the grand prize!

Equipment:

☐ Brewer(s) ☐ Kill-a-Watt meter ☐ Large insulated carafes ☐ Gong (optional!)

Activities:

☐ Part A – Brewing 0.975 liters of coffee in 45 minutes

☐ Part B – Blind taste test of everybody's coffee

Report:

☐ Video report of your final design

Summary of Contest Activities

There are two parts to the design contest. First, you'll have 45 minutes to brew almost 1 liter of coffee. Then, everybody will participate in the blind tasting. Before you leave, you will know the winning group!

Part A – Brewing 1 Liter of Coffee

As soon as you arrive in lab, wash your hands as usual, and feel free to organize your station and get your roasted beans out. Rinse your kettle with cool water if it's not already cool to the touch. DO NOT, however, begin to weigh anything, or grind anything, or heat any water. The contest coordinator will first give an overview of the contest guidelines and rules, and then ask for a volunteer to perform the ceremonial ringing of the gong. As soon as the gong rings, your group has 45 minutes to make your coffee! Each group will be provided with a thermally insulated carafe that will hold your 0.975 liters of brewed coffee. (This volume is based on the Zojirushi carafe maximum capacity.)

First, zero your Kill-a-Watt meter. Any device you use **must** be plugged into the meter and not re-zeroed until you complete your brew. While you are brewing, continue to measure your energy usage, and completely fill out your energy scoring sheet.

If you have extra beans, it's a good idea to do a test grind to make sure the grind size is what you want for the competition, and also to flush out any residual grounds.

After you're done with the 1 L, take a quick sample to get the overall TDS and overall PE. If you combined different brew types each might have a different PE, but this measurement will let you know what you ended up with.

Design Competition Energy Scoring Sheet

Group name: _____

Station number: _____   **Section number:** _____

Roast A (bean type): _____   **Roast B** (bean type): _____

Mass of green beans: _____ *grams*   Mass of green beans: _____ *grams*

Mass of roasted beans: _____ *grams*   Mass of roasted beans: _____ *grams*

Energy to roast: _____ *kW-hr*   Energy to roast: _____ *kW-hr*

Energy to roast per gram roasted bean: Energy to roast per gram roasted bean:

_____ ÷ _____ = _____ *kW-hr/gram*   _____ ÷ _____ = _____ *kW-hr/gram*

Actual mass of beans used: _____ *grams*   Actual mass of beans used: _____ *grams*

Energy per gram × total grams used: Energy per gram × total grams used:

_____ × _____ = _____ *kW-hr*   _____ × _____ = _____ *kW-hr*

Total energy for roasted coffee actually used in brew (Roast A + Roast B):

_____ + _____ = _____ *kW-hr*

Total mass of water heated: _____ *grams*

Initial Water Temp: _____ °C   Final Water Temp: _____ °C

Energy used to heat water: _____ *kW-hr*

Brewing method: _____

Mass of empty carafe: _____ *grams*   Mass of filled carafe: _____ *grams*

Mass of brew: _____ − _____ = _____ *grams*

(If the brew mass is more than 975 grams (0.975 liter), the energy penalty is zero.)

Deficient mass: __975__ − _____ = _____ *grams*

Energy penalty: _____ *grams* × __0.002__ *kW-hr/gram* = _____ *kW-hr*

Total energy used to produce your coffee (roast energy + water energy + penalty):

_____ + _____ + _____ = _____ *kW-hr*

(The contest coordinator will fill out the blind taste score and final score.)

Blind Taste Score: _____   **Final Score:** _____ $(kW\text{-}hr)^{-1}$

Design Competition Energy Scoring Sheet (Extra Copy)

Group name: _____

Station number: _____   **Section number:** _____

Roast A (bean type): _____   **Roast B** (bean type): _____

Mass of green beans: _____ *grams*   Mass of green beans: _____ *grams*

Mass of roasted beans: _____ *grams*   Mass of roasted beans: _____ *grams*

Energy to roast: _____ *kW-hr*   Energy to roast: _____ *kW-hr*

Energy to roast per gram roasted bean: Energy to roast per gram roasted bean:

_____ ÷ _____ = _____ *kW-hr/gram*   _____ ÷ _____ = _____ *kW-hr/gram*

Actual mass of beans used: _____ *grams* Actual mass of beans used: _____ *grams*

Energy per gram × total grams used: Energy per gram × total grams used:

_____ × _____ = _____ *kW-hr*   _____ × _____ = _____ *kW-hr*

Total energy for roasted coffee actually used in brew (Roast A + Roast B):

_____ + _____ = _____ *kW-hr*

Total mass of water heated: _____ *grams*

Initial Water Temp: _____ °C   Final Water Temp: _____ °C

Energy used to heat water: _____ *kW-hr*

Brewing method: _____

Mass of empty carafe: _____ *grams*   Mass of filled carafe: _____ *grams*

Mass of brew: _____ − _____ = _____ *grams*

(If the brew mass is more than 975 grams (0.975 liter), the energy penalty is zero.)

Deficient mass: 975   − _____ = _____ *grams*

Energy penalty: _____ *grams* × 0.002 *kW-hr/gram* = _____ *kW-hr*

Total energy used to produce your coffee (roast energy + water energy + penalty):

_____ + _____ + _____ = _____ *kW-hr*

(The contest coordinator will fill out the blind taste score and final score.)

Blind Taste Score: _____   **Final Score:** _____ $(kW\text{-}hr)^{-1}$

TDS Data for your Contest Brew (optional but a good idea)

Total mass of all coffee grounds used to brew 1 L: _____ *grams*

Mass of all brew in carafe: _____ *grams*

TDS: _____ %   PE: _____ × _____ ÷ _____ = _____ %

As soon as you're done, bring both your filled carafe and completed energy sheet to the contest coordinator. Once all of the carafes are submitted, the carafes will be randomized by assigning a random letter known only to the contest coordinator.

Part B – The Blind Taste Test

After the randomized carafes are brought back out, it's time to taste. You'll have about 45 minutes to taste the coffee in each carafe. Everybody will taste every carafe, and each group will *collectively* decide on a score for each of the sensory attributes. (For example, your group will submit 12 scores for 12 carafes.) Refer to Lab 0 for a reminder on how each of the attributes is defined.

For each tasting, dispense only about 1 ounce (half an espresso glass)... that's all you need. In fact, a small sip or two of each is all that's necessary. Discard any remaining coffee. It's recommended that you drink some water in between coffees to help prevent 'taste fatigue.' Some people find it useful to bring some plain crackers to help cleanse the palate.

For our purposes, high numbers are always better. In the case of acidity, for example, don't give a high score if the coffee is unpleasant because it's extremely sour – that would be a low score. Likewise, a dull flat coffee without any acidity is also a low score. Give a high acidity score if the acidity is pleasantly 'bright' without being overwhelming.

As soon as your group is done tasting, submit your score sheet to the TA, who will then go back and compile all the scores. You can clean up your station and take additional pictures or video while you're waiting. Before you leave, our volunteer will ring the gong again, and the winning groups will be announced. With good luck – and good engineering design – your group might be the one moving on to the championship round!

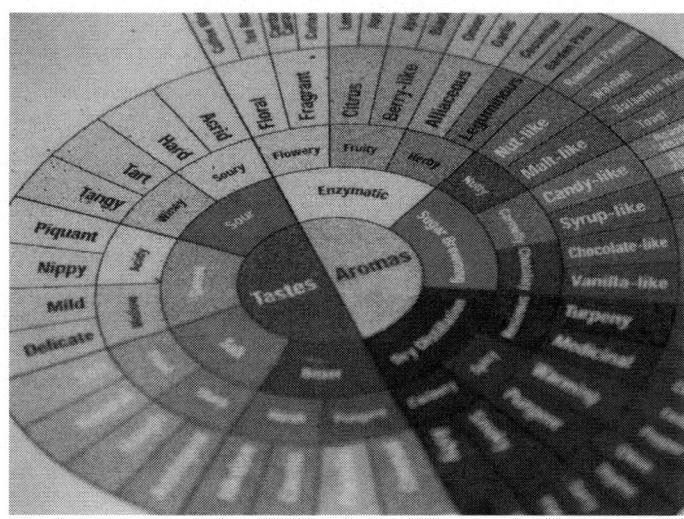

Design Competition Tasting Score Sheet

Group name: _____

Station number: _____   **Section number**: _____

All categories are ranked 1 to 10 (1=terrible, 10=excellent), except balance, which is ranked –10 (gut wrenching terrible) to +5 (excellent).

Carafe	A
Fragrance	
Acidity	
Flavor	
Body	
Aftertaste	
Balance	
Total	

Carafe	B
Fragrance	
Acidity	
Flavor	
Body	
Aftertaste	
Balance	
Total	

Carafe	C
Fragrance	
Acidity	
Flavor	
Body	
Aftertaste	
Balance	
Total	

Carafe	D
Fragrance	
Acidity	
Flavor	
Body	
Aftertaste	
Balance	
Total	

Carafe	E
Fragrance	
Acidity	
Flavor	
Body	
Aftertaste	
Balance	
Total	

Carafe	F
Fragrance	
Acidity	
Flavor	
Body	
Aftertaste	
Balance	
Total	

Carafe	G
Fragrance	
Acidity	
Flavor	
Body	
Aftertaste	
Balance	
Total	

Carafe	H
Fragrance	
Acidity	
Flavor	
Body	
Aftertaste	
Balance	
Total	

Carafe	I
Fragrance	
Acidity	
Flavor	
Body	
Aftertaste	
Balance	
Total	

Carafe	J
Fragrance	
Acidity	
Flavor	
Body	
Aftertaste	
Balance	
Total	

Carafe	K
Fragrance	
Acidity	
Flavor	
Body	
Aftertaste	
Balance	
Total	

Carafe	L
Fragrance	
Acidity	
Flavor	
Body	
Aftertaste	
Balance	
Total	

Design Competition Tasting Score Sheet (Extra Copy)

Group name: _____

Station number: _____ **Section number**: _____

All categories are ranked 1 to 10 (1=terrible, 10=excellent), except balance, which is ranked –10 (gut wrenching terrible) to +5 (excellent).

Carafe	A
Fragrance	
Acidity	
Flavor	
Body	
Aftertaste	
Balance	
Total	

Carafe	B
Fragrance	
Acidity	
Flavor	
Body	
Aftertaste	
Balance	
Total	

Carafe	C
Fragrance	
Acidity	
Flavor	
Body	
Aftertaste	
Balance	
Total	

Carafe	D
Fragrance	
Acidity	
Flavor	
Body	
Aftertaste	
Balance	
Total	

Carafe	E
Fragrance	
Acidity	
Flavor	
Body	
Aftertaste	
Balance	
Total	

Carafe	F
Fragrance	
Acidity	
Flavor	
Body	
Aftertaste	
Balance	
Total	

Carafe	G
Fragrance	
Acidity	
Flavor	
Body	
Aftertaste	
Balance	
Total	

Carafe	H
Fragrance	
Acidity	
Flavor	
Body	
Aftertaste	
Balance	
Total	

Carafe	I
Fragrance	
Acidity	
Flavor	
Body	
Aftertaste	
Balance	
Total	

Carafe	J
Fragrance	
Acidity	
Flavor	
Body	
Aftertaste	
Balance	
Total	

Carafe	K
Fragrance	
Acidity	
Flavor	
Body	
Aftertaste	
Balance	
Total	

Carafe	L
Fragrance	
Acidity	
Flavor	
Body	
Aftertaste	
Balance	
Total	

Lab Report: Final Design Video

No regular lab report is necessary for Lab 9. Instead, as described in detail on page XX, you and your group will submit a video that presents your final design. The following checklist is provided for your convenience.

Design Video Checklist

Video contents:

☐ Your group name, individual names, ID numbers, and section number (if applicable)

☐ Process flow diagram, with enough detail for others to replicate your process

☐ Mass balances, for water and coffee solids, including waste streams

☐ Type of beans and roast level(s)

☐ Energy usages for each step, and your logic for energy minimization

☐ TDS and PE for one of your final design brews (or competition brew)

☐ Overview of sensory evaluations as judged in the blind tasting

☐ Summary of what you would do in a future hypothetical contest to improve

Video format:

☐ Includes sufficient audio narration and / or subtitles to explain visuals

☐ Is less than five minutes total duration

☐ Is submitted as an MPG or a YouTube link

Finally, when you are done with your video, we recommend you sit back with a nice cup of freshly brewed coffee and reflect on all of the engineering and science concepts you have learned about during this course. Hopefully you have a better sense now of how to think like an engineer – and how to make excellent coffee!

Appendix A – General Guidelines for Brewing

For those of you who are less experienced coffee brewers, the information below provides a quick and handy summary of "Coffee Basics" and "General Rules of Brewing". Coffee basics covers general information about getting the best results by starting with good quality roasted beans and water. The general rules of brewing are based on common taste perception and preferences. As you work through the labs and explore your own personal taste preferences, keep these general rules of brewing in mind in order to more rapidly optimize towards your own individual "nirvana in a cup." Happy brewing.

Coffee Basics

- Use freshly roasted whole beans: To make good coffee you need to use fresh beans. After roasting, the coffee is at its best a couple of days after roasting and up to two weeks if stored properly. Roasted coffee should be stored in an airtight one way valve bag. Note: do not brew beans for at least 1-2 days after roasting. Chemical reactions continue after roasting that are crucial for the flavor and aroma profile.
- Grind immediately before brewing: Grinding releases trapped volatile components. That great smell of freshly roasted coffee means you are losing those great flavor molecules rapidly, so use ground coffee immediately. Ground coffee becomes stale within a few hours of grinding. The smaller the grind, the more rapid the loss. For example, a fine espresso grind will be stale within a few minutes.
- Use good water: water is almost 99% of brewed coffee. The coffee stuff in your cup is only a little more than 1% of the total, so starting with good water is essential.
- Use the right "brew ratio" and the proper grind size: The right ratio of water to ground coffee and the grind size are based on the brewing method. The goal is to optimize the extraction of the good flavors without over-extracting the bad flavors.

General Rules of Brewing

- Ratio of ground coffee to water: For an automatic drip or pour over method of brewing a water to coffee ratio of 15 to 20 grams of water to every gram of ground coffee is typically recommended.
- Water temperature: The suggested water temperature range is 90-95°C (194-203°F).
- Grind size: A narrow particle size helps with an even brewing extraction and more consistent brewing results. The grind should also be optimized to the type of brewing method. For example, espresso uses a very fine grind while a French press uses a coarser grind.
- Extraction time: Typically, most brewing methods use 2-6 minutes (espresso is about 30 seconds). The goal is to extract 18-22% of the ground coffee mass into the brew to obtain 1.15-1.35% total dissolved coffee solids or stuff in the brewed coffee. (You study this in more detail in Labs 5 and 7!)

Appendix B – Useful Units and Conversions for Coffee

Mass & volume conversions for <u>water</u> at room temperature

1 milliliter water = 1 gram   (1 mL = 1 g)

1 liter = 1000 milliliters = 1000 grams = 1 kilogram   (1 L = 1000 mL = 1000 g = 1 kg)

1 cup = 235 grams

1 cup = 8 fluid ounces

1 fluid ounce of water = 29.6 grams

4.25 cups of water = 1000 grams = 1 liter

Temperature

To convert from Celsius to Fahrenheit, multiply by 9/5 and add 32.
To convert from Fahrenheit to Celsius, subtract 32 and multiply the difference by 5/9.

°C	0	10	20	30	40	50	60	70	80	90	100	110	120
°F	32	50	68	86	104	122	140	158	176	194	212	230	248

°C	130	140	150	160	170	180	190	200	210	220	230	240	250
°F	266	284	302	320	338	356	374	392	410	428	446	464	482

Brew Ratio Table

	Desired Brew Ratio						
Mass of Dry Grounds (grams)	14	15	16	17	18	19	20
5	70	75	80	85	90	95	100
10	140	150	160	170	180	190	200
15	210	225	240	255	270	285	300
20	280	300	320	340	360	380	400
25	350	375	400	425	450	475	500
30	420	450	480	510	540	570	600
35	490	525	560	595	630	665	700
40	560	600	640	680	720	760	800
45	630	675	720	765	810	855	900
50	700	750	800	850	900	950	1000

Mass of Water to Use (grams)

Appendix C – Tips on Data Analysis and Plotting

A crucial skill, regardless of your career path, involves the analysis and communication of data. Even if you become an award-winning author or artist, you need to be able to understand your royalties – a kind of financial data. The lab reports in "The Design of Coffee" are aimed at developing your expertise in analyzing and plotting scientific data, with a focus on using standard spreadsheet software (e.g., Microsoft Excel). The skills are translatable to other types of data as well (if you can plot temperature versus time, you can plot royalty income versus time). In this appendix we summarize some helpful tips to perform the necessary data analysis, and to make your plots easily understandable by others.

We focus here on three topics: recording data, plotting data, and performing linear regressions (or "best fits") of data.

Tips on Recording Data

Examine below the two examples of an Excel spreadsheet. Both of them contain exactly the same data, but hopefully you agree that there is a tremendous difference in clarity and legibility. Specifically, the one on the left is an example of "bad practices (what *not* to do!), while the right is an example of good practices.

You can see most of the differences visually, but for the sake of clarity some of the basic good practices for recording and analyzing data are as follows

1) **Units.** The most important rule: when you put down numbers in a spreadsheet, it should be obvious to any other reader what the units are. (There is a huge difference between grams or kilograms!) Always clearly label the units at the top of a column (or somewhere else very clear).

2) **Labels.** Along with the units, some descriptive label (e.g., "Time") for each column of data is necessary.

3) **Metadata.** It is good practice to place some information about the data at the top of the spreadsheet, including for example the type of data, who took it, when, where, etc. Also give descriptive names to your workbook and all worksheets. "Mydata" could mean anything, whereas "coffee_pH_trial_3" is extremely specific.

4) **Significant digits.** It is easy in Excel to include way too many digits. Don't include seven or eight digits in a number if only the first 3 are significant.

5) **Formulas.** Any constants that are used in calculations should be clearly entered and labeled nearby *with appropriate units*. Then, your calculations should refer to the cell containing that constant. (In Excel, you use the $ prefactor to hold the cell fixed in a formula.)

(Bad Practice)

18.0	fine	
	1	2
0.5	4.8000	4.5000
2.0	4.1080	3.7113
4.0	3.8298	3.1460
6.0	3.5421	2.6575
8.0	2.8952	1.8771
10.0	2.9921	1.8926

(Good Practice)

Caffeine Experiment, Trials 1 & 2		
12-Jul-15	2:30pm	
Experiments by J. Lee & A. Gomez		
Brewing Ratio:		18
Grind size:		Fine
	Trial 1	Trial 2
	(25°C)	(90°C)
Time	Caffeine Concentration	
[minutes]	[g / L]	[g / L]
0.5	4.8	4.5
2	4.1	3.7
4	3.8	3.1
6	3.5	2.7
8	2.9	1.9
10	3.0	1.9

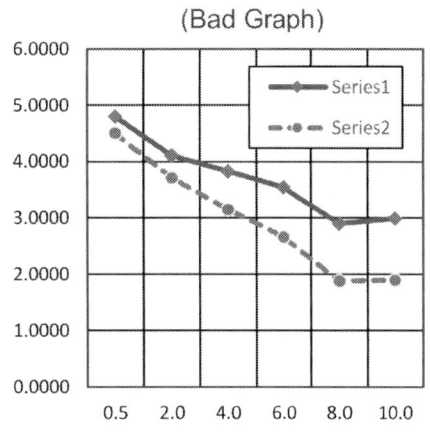
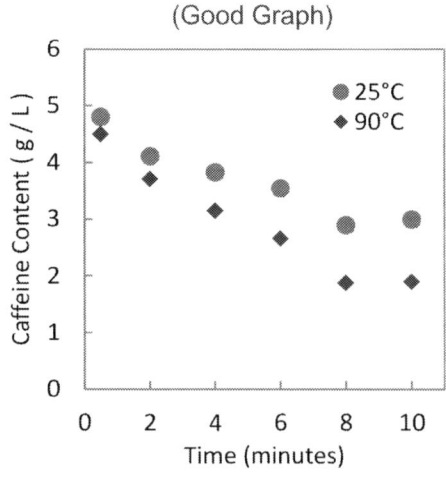

Tips on Plotting Data

Examine the two graphs above: they have the same info, but one is clearly better. When graphing data, it's traditional to always state the plot as "y" versus "x", so that a plot of "mass" vs. "time" will have mass on the vertical axis and time on the horizontal axis. Good practices for plotting data include the following.

1) **Axes labels.** The worst possible mistake is to forget to label what the horizontal and vertical axes represent. How else will the viewer know what they're looking at?

2) **Units.** Again, include the units on the axes labels (and legend if appropriate).

3) **Legend.** If your plot includes multiple trials or conditions, use a legend to differentiate them. Make sure each curve has a descriptive label. "Series 1" means nothing!

4) **Markers vs. lines**. The standard convention is to use individual markers to represent individual experimental measurements. Don't connect them with a line (even though that's the default in Excel). Only use solid lines for best fits or for modeling.

5) **Visibility.** Use bold and bright colors for your data. It is difficult to see yellow on white.

6) **Aesthetics.** Most people find a gray background and/or horizontal gridlines quite "ugly" and distracting. You are urged to get rid of the gridlines and use a simple white background. The focus should be on the data – not the background.

Procedure to Perform a "Best Fit" to your Data

Oftentimes we are interested in calculating the slope of your data, which is just another way of asking "how quickly does my data change with respect to some variable?" For example, in Lab 3 you have to determine the slope of the pH versus time. There are several ways to calculate the line that best fits the data (also known as linear regression), but the easiest way in Excel (2013) is to follow this procedure. First, plot your data in a standard scatter plot. Click on your plot, then select "Add Chart Element." One of the options should be "Trend line", and select the series of data you want to fit. A best fit line will appear on the graph. Click on the line, and select "Format Trend line," then click "Display Equation on Chart." An equation of the form $y = mx + b$ will appear on the chart. The slope you want is the m value. If you are comfortable using functions in Excel, you can instead use the "slope" function directly in the spreadsheet itself (so that you don't clutter up your graph).

Further Reading

The Design of Coffee: An Engineering Approach is intended as an introduction to coffee, with a focus on thinking about coffee from an engineering perspective. For readers interested in diving deeper into the rich science of coffee, we recommend the following books.

Coffee Technology, by Michael Sivetz & Norman Desrosier (1979)

Considered by many in the coffee industry as the "Bible of Coffee," this classic is difficult to find (used copies are available on Amazon for $900!). But if you do get a copy, it is a wealth of information written by a chemical engineer (Sivetz) with tremendous experience in the design and operation of coffee roasteries.

Coffee, volumes 1 through 6, edited by R. J. Clarke and R. Macrae (1987)

This highly technical collection covers the full range of coffee science in great detail. Volumes 1 and 2 focus on coffee chemistry and coffee technology respectively. Volumes 3 and 4 focus on coffee biology, and volumes 5 and 6 focus on related beverages and commercial/legal aspects of coffee.

Coffee: Recent Developments, edited by R. J. Clarke and O. G. Vitzthum (2001)

An updated and condensed (but still highly technical) version of *Coffee* by Clarke and Macrae.

Espresso Coffee: The Science of Quality, edited by Andrea Illy & Rinantonio Viani (2005)

IllyCaffé is one of the leading producers of high quality espresso in the world. This book, co-edited by Andrea Illy (grandson of founder Francesco Illy) covers all aspects of coffee science, from coffee agronomy to human nutrition, with a focus on espresso coffee. Mandatory reading for anybody serious about coffee.

Uncommon Grounds, by Mark Pendergrast (2010)

For those interested in the social and economic aspects of coffee, this book dives deep into the history of coffee, from its discovery in Africa, to the colonial period, to mass consumer culture of the twentieth century, to modern "third wave" café culture.

Water for Coffee, by Maxwell Colonna-Dashwood & Christopher Hendon (2015)

As you've learned, coffee is about 99% water... and not all water is created equal! Recent research has demonstrated that the chemical composition of trace ions in the water can alter the details of the extraction. This book provides a great overview of water chemistry and how it affects the flavor of coffee.

Made in the USA
San Bernardino, CA
20 April 2017